Improving Management of the Public Work Force

The Challenge to State and Local Government

A Statement on National Policy
by the Research and Policy Committee
of the Committee for Economic Development

NOVEMBER 1978

Library of Congress Cataloging in Publication Data

Committee for Economic Development.
  Improving management of the public work force.

    1. Civil service—United States—States.
2. Local officials and employees—United States.
3. Personnel management—United States. 4. Employee-
management relations in government—United States.
I. Title.
JK2465.C63 1978   353.001   78-11075
ISBN 0-87186-067-8

First printing: November 1978
Paperbound: $5.00
Library binding: $6.50
Printed in the United States of America by Georgian Press, Inc.
Design: Harry Carter

COMMITTEE FOR ECONOMIC DEVELOPMENT
477 Madison Avenue, New York, N.Y. 10022
1700 K Street, N.W. Washington, D.C. 20006

Contents

Improving Management of the Public Work Force

The Challenge to State and Local Government

Responsibility for CED Statements on National Policy

The Committee for Economic Development is an independent research and educational organization of two hundred business executives and educators. CED is nonprofit, nonpartisan, and nonpolitical. Its purpose is to propose policies that will help to bring about steady economic growth at high employment and reasonably stable prices, increase productivity and living standards, provide greater and more equal opportunity for every citizen, and improve the quality of life for all. A more complete description of CED is to be found on page 138.

All CED policy recommendations must have the approval of the Research and Policy Committee, trustees whose names are listed on page 3. This Committee is directed under the bylaws to "initiate studies into the principles of business policy and of public policy which will foster the full contribution by industry and commerce to the attainment and maintenance" of the objectives stated above. The bylaws emphasize that "all research is to be thoroughly objective in character, and the approach in each instance is to be from the standpoint of the general welfare and not from that of any special political or economic group." The Committee is aided by a Research Advisory Board of leading social scientists and by a small permanent professional staff.

The Research and Policy Committee is not attempting to pass judgment on any pending specific legislative proposals; its purpose is to urge careful consideration of the objectives set forth in this statement and of the best means of accomplishing those objectives.

Each statement is preceded by extensive discussions, meetings, and exchanges of memoranda. The research is undertaken by a subcommittee, assisted by advisors chosen for their competence in the field under study. The members and advisors of the subcommittee that prepared this statement are listed on page 4.

The full Research and Policy Committee participates in the drafting of findings and recommendations. Likewise, the trustees on the drafting subcommittee vote to approve or disapprove a policy statement, and they share with the Research and Policy Committee the privilege of submitting individual comments for publication, as noted on pages 3 and 4 and on the appropriate page of the text of the statement.

Except for the members of the Research and Policy Committee and the responsible subcommittee, the recommendations presented herein are not necessarily endorsed by other trustees or by the advisors, contributors, staff members, or others associated with CED.

3

Purpose of This Statement

IN 1976, CED PUBLISHED *Improving Productivity in State and Local Government*, which addressed the broad issue of how to keep down the rising cost of the state-local sector without crippling important public services. In that statement, we underscored the importance of people as a major source of productivity improvement in government and indicated that we would produce a follow-up statement dealing more specifically with problems of managing personnel and developing human resources in government. This statement, *Improving Management of the Public Work Force: The Challenge to State and Local Government*, is that follow-up.

Our interest in state and local government productivity stems principally from CED studies of inflation undertaken in the late sixties and early seventies. Some of our trustees were startled to realize how rapidly the state-local sector was growing, and it became clear that the implications of that growth for impeding economic development and contributing to inflation were profound. Our work on fiscal and monetary policy, dating back to the 1940s, focused largely on the role of the federal government in promoting growth and curbing inflation. Although that concern continues, we have become more conscious of the size and performance of state and local government as they relate to the nation's major economic problems.

Growth in State and Local Government

Total government expenditures in 1977 were $621 billion, a sum equivalent to 32.9 percent of the gross national product. Although federal expenditures were $423 billion, $170 billion of that total was in the form of transfer payments to individuals; $68 billion was passed on as grants to state and local governments. Actual purchase of goods and services by the federal government was $145 billion, or 7.7 percent of GNP (two-thirds of which was for defense); whereas state-local government purchases totaled $245 billion, or 13.2 percent of GNP. The fact is that although the federal government collects and distributes enormous amounts of tax money, the preponderance of government administration (about 80 percent of nondefense purchases of goods and services) takes place at the state and local levels. That heavy weight of administrative responsibility is reflected in employment figures: The federal civilian work force was 2.7 million in 1977; whereas the state-local work force was more than 12 million, or more than four times as great.

Public Concern with Government Cost and Performance

Recently, the concern for curbing costs and promoting effective performance of state and local government has become a major public issue. The taxpayer's revolt (which has had its greatest impact at the state and local levels, with the passage of Proposition 13 in California) and the rising incidence of public-employee strikes have all contributed to this concern. The newly enacted Civil Service Reform Act of 1978 reflects public concern over the size of government budgets and payrolls at all levels. Although our statement is timely in this regard, we want to emphasize that we have not written it in response to the current surge of public reaction over the cost and performance of public employees. It is an issue the importance of which we anticipated through clearly observable trends years ago.

The current public fervor over rising taxes, the perceived wastefulness in the spending of tax money, and government performance in general should come as no surprise. The trends producing this climate were observable years ago and prompted our studies on government productivity and personnel management. We have attempted to approach the topic dispassionately and to suggest a practical approach that acknowledges problems without assigning blame. Our interest is to indicate to political and government leaders how they can take action to make needed improvements.

A Comprehensive Approach

We take a broad view of the issue of managing the public work force. It is an economic concern because of the enormous sums of money and real human resources involved. It is a political concern because the goals of government are set through the political process and because public employees participate actively in politics. It is a managerial concern because many government agencies are large, complex organizations facing difficult managerial problems. And it is a distinctly human concern because the services provided by state and local government— education, police and fire protection, water and sewer facilities, social and health services, and many others—are so crucial to modern life.

Our approach attempts to account for those many dimensions and to determine how they interact with one another, rather than focus narrowly on any one aspect of public personnel management. We hope, in fact, that the principal purpose served by this statement will be to underscore the importance of dealing with public personnel management in a comprehensive fashion that takes into account all its component parts and is sensitive to how they affect one another.

Both this report and the appended comments of individual trustees highlight the importance of making collective bargaining, wherever it exists in the public sector, an effective instrument in setting public employment compensation at equitable and competitive levels. All too easily, government wage settlements can degenerate into an inflationary spiral of wage-tax-cost increases. There is urgent need to develop counterbalancing forces in the public sector that are equivalent to the counterbalancing collective bargaining forces supplied in the private sector by the market and by profit discipline.

I would call attention to two particular recommendations in our report that could contribute to improved performance by state and local governments in this area: greater professionalism on the part of government negotiators and the communication to the taxpayers of estimated budgetary consequences of proposed settlements. But for these suggestions to be of much help, a spirit of better management needs to pervade the whole fabric of government. That, we believe, can provide a basis for better long-run understanding between government officials and employees. A number of the recommendations in that statement will work toward that end. We urge more constructive dialogue among informed representatives of all the key interests involved to achieve further progress in this issue.

Practical Problems of Implementation

We are not proposing the simple transfer of private-sector practices of labor relations and personnel administration to the public sector. We have attempted to glean from the experience of the business people who studied the issue ways in which government practice could be improved, but always with a recognition of the important distinctions between business and government. And we have relied heavily on the experience and advice of practitioners in government who represent both management and labor, without whom we would not have attempted such a study.

Our proposals are not equally applicable to the highly diverse state and local governments across the nation. Nor are we suggesting implementation of our recommendations without careful thought to the special circumstances of each jurisdiction. Many government practitioners will agree with our proposals but will face formidable political and organizational problems in implementation. For them, we hope the statement provides support as much as guidance.

For others, either in government or outside it, who see problems in personnel management but have not had the time to think through all their implications, we hope the framework laid out in this statement—which discusses and relates such key topics as the political economy of public employment, personnel structures, collective bargaining, the role of managers, and performance and satisfaction in the workplace—will prove useful as a statement of goals and an agenda for improvement.

Special Contributions

The subcommittee that prepared this statement included a number of trustees and nontrustee members with extensive experience in government and industrial labor relations and personnel management. It was ably assisted by an impressive panel of advisors from academic institutions, labor organizations, and public policy study groups. I wish particularly to express our appreciation to our labor advisors, who helped the subcommittee with their insights even if it sometimes reached conclusions with which they disagreed. A list of all subcommittee members and designated advisors appears on page 4. In addition, the group benefited from the informal comments of a sizable number of experts in government and related fields on various points at issue, and our thanks are extended to them.

I pay special tribute to the wise guidance of the chairman of the subcommittee, Rocco C. Siciliano, chairman and chief executive officer of TICOR, Los Angeles, and former Under Secretary of Commerce, Assistant Secretary of Labor, and Special Assistant for Personnel Management to President Eisenhower. Wayne E. Thompson, senior vice president of the Dayton Hudson Corporation, who served as vice chairman of the subcommittee and who chaired the CED subcommittee on state and local government productivity, brought his valuable background as city manager of both Richmond and Oakland, California, to the project. Special recognition is also due R. Scott Fosler, director of government studies at CED and the project director of this report, for his unusual skill in weaving together a comprehensive consideration of the many interrelated facets of this important and complex subject.

Franklin A. Lindsay, *Chairman*
Research and Policy Committee

Chapter 1

INTRODUCTION AND SUMMARY

A HIGH-QUALITY CIVIL SERVICE IS ESSENTIAL to effective and efficient operations at all levels of government. Yet, in recent years, there has been growing concern over the performance and cost of the public work force. (See Appendix A.) In the past, this Committee has recommended improvements in the personnel system at the federal level,[1] many of which are embodied in the newly enacted Civil Service Reform Act of 1978. We believe it is now equally important to address the problems that have developed in the substantially larger and more rapidly growing state and local government work force.*

State and local governments employed more than 12 million people in 1977, or more than four times the 2.7 million federal civilian employees (see Figure 1). Whereas federal employment has increased by only 23 percent in the past twenty years, state-local employment has soared by 132 percent and now accounts for one of seven U.S. workers in nonagricultural establishments (see Figure 2). If the cost of government is to be restrained without sacrificing important public services, and if

---

1. See, for example, *Revitalizing the Federal Personnel System* (1978).

*See memorandum by W. D. DANCE, page 126.

12

performance is to be enhanced, political and government leaders must take the initiative to improve the management of the public work force at the state and local levels.

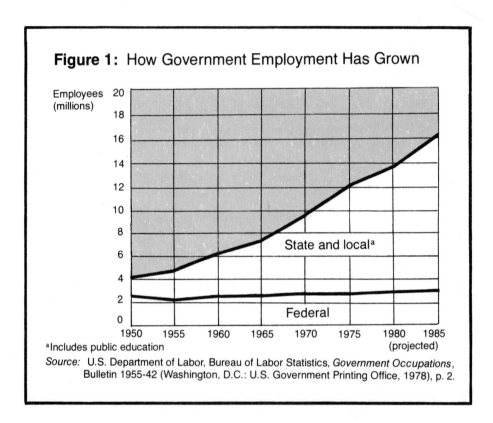

Figure 1: How Government Employment Has Grown

Employees (millions)

State and local[a]

Federal

1950 1955 1960 1965 1970 1975 1980 1985
(projected)

[a]Includes public education

Source: U.S. Department of Labor, Bureau of Labor Statistics, *Government Occupations*, Bulletin 1955-42 (Washington, D.C.: U.S. Government Printing Office, 1978), p. 2.

TENSION BETWEEN TAXPAYERS AND PUBLIC EMPLOYEES

The taxpayer's revolt epitomized by the passage of Proposition 13 in California has focused attention on the number of public employees and the level of their wages and benefits. Taxpayers also increasingly feel that they are not getting their money's worth from the services provided by government, and here again, public employees often bear the brunt of the criticism. The increasing incidence of strikes and disruptions of public services has caused public irritation and alarm and has created ill will toward government workers in general.

The response of public employees has been mixed. Some are leaving government for higher pay, prestige, or satisfaction in private employment; those whose jobs have few counterparts in the private sector feel caught and resentful; and many are resolved to fight through political action for what they perceive to be adequate pay and working conditions. There are, in short, disturbing signs of sagging morale.

EFFECTIVE MANAGEMENT OF
THE PUBLIC WORK FORCE

We view these developments with concern. In *Improving Productivity in State and Local Government* (1976), we noted the rapid growth in the state-local sector and suggested a direction for curbing costs without sacrificing important public services. We concluded that the failure both to improve effectiveness and efficiency of public services and to achieve economical use of public money cannot be explained away by the presumed deficiencies of public employees. Rather, major sources of the problem are the lack of common purpose, the excessive political competition among numerous interest groups, and the related failure of top officials to provide effective management in government. We reaffirm that conclusion.

One of the most important ingredients of overall management is the effective utilization of people. This is especially true in the labor-intensive operations of government, in which improvements in productivity depend heavily on the performance of people rather than machines. However, personnel management in government is impeded by economic, political, and legal factors over which public-sector managers themselves may have little direct control.

Personnel policy in government, as in business, is affected by market forces. For example, pupil-teacher ratios in public schools are determined not only by educational standards but also by the cost of attracting the number and quality of teachers required to meet educational objectives. In many communities, more police officers, fire fighters, and other classes of public employees would be hired if the cost of employing them were lower.

However, within wide bounds, the economic constraints on governments are defined politically. The goals of government, the means of achieving those goals, and the willingness to pay for the personnel required to implement those means are all determined through the political process. Of course, public employees themselves are not neutral bystanders in that political process. They participate actively, both as individuals and through their organizations, by supporting candidates for public office and lobbying for favorable government policy.

Government managers must not only work within these economic and political constraints but must also face legal and administrative rigidities in personnel practice that often unduly limit their ability to hire, train, assign, motivate, and dismiss employees. Many state and local governments attempt to operate with multiple, overlapping, or fragmented personnel systems, including patronage, merit or civil service systems, and collective bargaining. Each system can pose obstacles to effective management, and each, if not properly structured, can conflict with the others.

COHERENT FRAMEWORK
FOR PUBLIC PERSONNEL MANAGEMENT

If government officials are to be held accountable for results, they must be provided with a personnel system that is comprehensive and conducive to a high level of performance. Such a system must be structured in a manner that recognizes the economic and political environment in which government functions. For example, compensation plans, whether established through law or in negotiated contracts, need to be more precisely attuned to the fiscal constraints on government. Collective bargaining structures that fail to take into account the inherently political nature of collective bargaining in government will produce needless frictions and can unnecessarily tie the hands of management. It is particularly important that government personnel policy deal practically with the fact that workers can, and increasingly do, engage in job actions that can disrupt public services.

Personnel systems must also assure internal consistency and compatibility among their key components. It is not enough to perfect the techniques of selecting employees or classifying jobs, although those important technical functions of a good merit system need attention. Merit systems must also take into account the realities of collective bargaining. Collective bargaining, where adopted, must be attuned to the overriding priority of preserving merit principles in government and must be closely linked to the realities of managing public agencies. Effective personnel management also requires sensitivity to the changing character and desires of employees and skill in the day-to-day management of people.

Fashioning a cohesive personnel system that deals with these relationships is not a simple task, especially in the politically volatile atmosphere of government. It should begin with a clear articulation of goals that emphasize effective and efficient public service and the fair treatment of public employees. The achievement of these goals will depend upon certain key factors:

- personnel policy that distinguishes among the roles of top policy makers, professional managers, and other employees

- personnel procedures and practices based on merit that are supportive of management and that protect employee rights

Figure 2: Government and Private Employment in the United States, 1957 and 1977 (millions)

	1957	1977	Percent Increase
Federal government	2.2	2.7	22.7
State and local government	5.4	12.5	131.5
Private sector	45.3	66.9	47.7
Total nonagricultural employment	52.9	82.1	55.2

Note: Data are for wage and salary workers in nonagricultural establishments.

Source: Economic Report of the President (Washington, D.C.: U.S. Government Printing Office, January 1978).

● the structuring of collective bargaining, where it is adopted, to take into account the political nature of government

● the development of managerial capability as the key to effective personnel management

● special attention to and experimentation with various modes of agency operation to improve employee performance, job satisfaction, and personal development

GOALS FOR THE PUBLIC SERVICE

Over the years, the purpose of public service has become diffused by the growing size and complexity of government, the increased specialization of personnel functions, and the multiplicity of political goals associated with public employment. We are convinced that it is time to refocus attention on the principal purpose of public service—providing effective, efficient, economical, and fair government. We believe that state and local government personnel policy should emphasize the following priorities in support of that purpose.

Revitalizing the Merit Principle

Public employees should be selected, assigned, promoted, and compensated on the basis of ability and performance. Of course, some state governments and numerous local governments have never formally adopted the merit principle. But in many of those that have done so, the civil service or merit systems, initially conceived to promote the merit principle, have developed rigidities, such as overreliance on seniority, that impede the appropriate use of the most qualified people. Specialized personnel administration has at times been preoccupied with techniques that bear little relation to assuring that the best people are available for assignment. Collective bargaining has in many instances led management to agree to restrictions on the best use of employees' skills and potential. Discrimination on the basis of race, cultural background, sex, or other factors not related to the job has kept talented people from being hired and promoted. Action must be taken to check and reverse these tendencies.

Restoring the Authority of Managers to Manage

Managers should be given the authority and the resources to accomplish the objectives for which they are responsible and should then be held accountable for results. The accumulated maze of personnel restrictions is preventing government managers from doing their jobs or at the very least providing excuses for poor performance.

The style of management is not the issue here. The relative effectiveness of various styles or approaches to management depends largely upon the nature of the operation and the people involved. Whatever approach is taken, however, someone should be clearly designated to be responsible for results, and that person should be given adequate authority to ensure that the skills and energies of employees are used effectively to accomplish those results.

Protecting the Rights of Employees

Employees need to be protected from political abuse and arbitrary bureaucratic action. Protection of individual rights and respect for individual interests in employment are independent goals worthy in their own right. Moreover, effective and efficient government is best provided by employees who are secure in the knowledge that they will be judged on the basis of how well they serve the public and that they will be treated with fairness and dignity.

Enhancing Personal Performance, Development, and Job Satisfaction

Public personnel policy should be geared to enhancing performance, encouraging the development of individual capabilities, and improving the quality of working life. Many employees who are otherwise highly motivated are frustrated by bureaucratic impediments, lack of clear objectives, or inadequate feedback on their performance. In other instances, deficiencies in supervision result in the waste of employee time and talent. Public employees collectively represent a wealth of human capability that should be permitted and encouraged to develop fully. Jobs and the employment environment should be structured in a manner that is both productive for public services and satisfying and fulfilling to employees themselves.

STRUCTURE FOR PERSONNEL MANAGEMENT

Government personnel policy should not be restricted to any one class of employees. Rather, it should promote the personal development and effective use of all the people employed by government. However, appropriate policies and practices may vary according to the different roles and responsibilities of government employees.

● *Top Policy Makers.* Elected officials are selected directly by the public and usually appoint other top personnel to serve at their pleasure. The principal criterion guiding the selection and behavior of top policy officials is appropriately political. Nevertheless, public personnel policy should not neglect the development and best use of the analytic and managerial abilities and time of those in policy positions.

● *Professional Managers.* People in managerial positions bear the principal responsibility for the operation of government. They should be guided by, and judged primarily on, criteria of professional capability and performance. The conditions of their employment (hiring, compensation, assignment, promotion, and discharge) should be largely insulated from political considerations. At the same time, they should be subject to the direction of, and accountable to, top policy makers. An approach that balances these professional and political needs is required. Certain classes of professional, technical, and confidential employees should be treated similarly.

● *Other Employees.* A more formal personnel structure is required for the other employees of government, who constitute the greatest proportion of the public work force. At this level in particular, the laws and regulations of civil service and so-called merit systems have become rigid to the detriment of performance, and the advent of collective bargaining has tended to cause confusion and tension with more traditional personnel procedures.

We believe that although more effective use could be made of the time and talents of top policy makers, particularly elected officials, the judgment of their performance is for the most part the direct responsibility of the public. Some governments may opt for a separate personnel system for management and certain professional personnel. For the principal personnel system, which covers the major part of the public work force, we recommend the following adjustments:

● The various personnel support functions typically associated with civil service or merit systems, other aspects of personnel administration, and labor relations are integral to one another and should be consolidated in a single agency of the executive branch of government.

● A separate board should be created independent of the consolidated personnel agency to perform an appeals and investigatory function in assuring that the merit principle is upheld and employee rights are protected.

● Specific personnel practices should be revised to strengthen the emphasis on merit and performance in such areas as recruitment, selection, assignment, promotion, job classification, compensation, discipline, separation, performance appraisal, affirmative action, collective bargaining, and planning for future staffing needs.

● Formal mechanisms should be created to assure coordination among the various facets of government operation that affect personnel, including planning, finance, budget, management analysis, legal affairs, and line operations.

● The personnel management support functions (e.g., recruitment, selection, and classification) should be regularly evaluated to determine and enhance their effectiveness in meeting the broader purposes of government.

COLLECTIVE BARGAINING*

Collective bargaining between employees and the management representatives of state and local government has spread rapidly in the past fifteen years as employees have sought a more direct voice in determining the conditions of their employment. Those jurisdictions that already have collective bargaining should reassess its structure to make

*See memoranda by WILLIAM F. MAY and ROBERT R. NATHAN, pages 126 and 127.

certain that it supports effective and efficient government. In jurisdictions that do not have collective bargaining, public officials have the opportunity to take the lead in creating a positive atmosphere that public employees may find more attractive than collective bargaining. However, these jurisdictions should also realistically prepare to deal with the question of whether and how to adopt collective bargaining if events make such action necessary.

Private-sector models of collective bargaining cannot be wholly transplanted to the public sector. If it is to function effectively, collective bargaining in government must be designed to take into account the political environment in which it operates and to assure protection of the public interest for which government is responsible. Special care is required to assure that collective bargaining does not work at cross-purposes with merit systems and related personnel support functions. States should assume responsibility for establishing a clear legal framework for labor relations in their own government and in their subdivisions. In those instances in which states decide that collective bargaining is desirable, we urge that the following principles be considered in creating a workable structure sensitive to the rights and needs of both employees and the public:

- An impartial public-employee relations board should be established to oversee the structure and procedures for labor relations in both the state and its local governments. The substance of employee relations, including negotiations and the administration of contracts, would be primarily the responsibility of the executive branch of the state government and its subdivisions.

- In providing for the determination of bargaining units and the manner of representation, state law should fully take into account the protection of the public interest, the effectiveness and efficiency of current and future modes of operation, the legitimate interests of groups of employees and their organizations, and the individual rights of employees.

- Management should be represented in collective negotiations by the executive branch of the government. However, the legislative body has an interest and responsibility for assuring that agreements are in accord with the broader interpretation of the public interest, including fiscal limitations, and the rights of employees.

● In order to represent the government effectively, the executive branch should develop professional expertise in labor relations and should assure the effective coordination of all aspects of management related to personnel matters that are integral to collective bargaining.

● The process of bargaining in government should be structured so that the public is informed of the terms of employment under negotiation before settlement is reached and so that the full fiscal implications of settlements are clearly understood.

Resolving Impasses

It is a fact that labor disputes do occur. Therefore, if collective bargaining is to work, there must be provision for the fair and definitive resolution of impasses. Every effort should be made to provide the means for, and to develop the tradition of, reaching the peaceful settlement of public labor disputes. The best means of avoiding labor disputes is to anticipate and resolve potential problems before they lead to confrontation. This requires day-to-day attention by management and supervisory personnel to the needs and legitimate grievances of employees.

Responsibility for facilitating the resolution of impasses should be given to a neutral state agency that is professionally staffed, adequately compensated, and equipped with a range of mechanisms for settling, or facilitating the settlement of, public-sector labor disputes. These mechanisms should include but not necessarily be limited to mediation, fact-finding, and arbitration. In addition, states might provide for other resolution procedures, including public referendum and final resolution by the state legislature or local legislative body.

Public-Employee Strikes

For many critical public services, work stoppages or other job actions can threaten government's ability to protect the public health, safety, and welfare. Government has fundamental obligations to the public and should take action to ensure that strikes or other job actions by employees do not impede the meeting of those obligations. Summarily prohibiting strikes by employees may or may not be the best way of keeping strikes from occurring. But, in fact, legal prohibition of strikes does not address the question of how to deal with illegal work stoppages. Each state and local government needs to decide for itself how its policy regarding public-employee strikes, including the mix of legal prohibition and contingency planning, can best protect the public from crippling deprivation of public services. The objective is to avoid injurious disruptions of public services through whatever combination of legal prohibition of strikes, preparation to deal with strikes, and impasse-resolution techniques best suits local needs and is conducive to fair and workable labor relations.

ROLE OF THE MANAGER

Providing an appropriate structure for personnel management and labor relations can remove impediments but by itself will not guarantee high employee performance. It remains the responsibility of management to set objectives, mobilize resources, determine appropriate modes of operation, and motivate people to get the job done.

Achieving a high level of managerial performance in government depends upon the same factors that apply in business or other institutions: Managers themselves require direction, they must be capable, they must be given authority commensurate with their responsibility, and they should be given incentives to perform, including being held accountable for, and rewarded on the basis of, results.

Ability to Manage

Assuring the development of a cadre of capable managers depends chiefly upon the following measures:

- identifying people, both outside and inside government, with the potential for managing in the demanding environment of government and permitting top officials flexibility in assigning managers to positions in which their abilities can best be used

- paying compensation that is competitive with similar positions in the private sector and other governments

- providing training and educational opportunities for executive development

● treating managers with the respect and giving them the support commensurate with their formidable responsibilities

Authority to Manage

Without the authority to manage, even the most qualified manager will be prevented from doing his or her job. The structure for public-sector personnel management that we recommend would shift greater authority to managers and would underscore the responsibility of operating managers, rather than the personnel specialists, for the management of personnel in their agencies. Government managers possess no more authority than that granted to them by law or delegated by top policy officials. If elected executives or legislative leaders lack the necessary legal bases, political power, or willingness to delegate authority, it cannot be expected that managers themselves can muster the authority to manage in the politically volatile environment of government (unless, of course, they possess directing powers granted by law, unusual personal abilities, or independent bases of political support). We believe that the effectiveness of public-sector managers will be greatly enhanced if the following steps are taken:

● Managers should be given greater authority over such key personnel matters as recruiting, hiring, training, assigning, promoting, disciplining, compensating, and firing employees in accordance with government-wide standards of due process, merit, and employee protection.*

● Managers should be involved in collective bargaining with the employees for whom they are responsible, at least to the extent of advising management negotiators on bargaining items related to their operations.

Incentive to Manage

If managers are to be given greater authority to do their jobs, they should also be held more strictly accountable for results. Greater stress should be placed on developing the performance measures and means of evaluation by which government performance and, consequently, individual managerial performance can be assessed. Top policy officials

*See memorandum by CHARLES P. BOWEN, JR., page 128.

should have sufficient legal authority to determine managers' compensation, promotion, and continuation in public service on the basis of such performance appraisals.

Middle Management and Supervision

A chronic weak point in government is the middle manager or supervisor who is closest to operating-level public employees and who bears the principal responsibility for making the machinery of government work. Government should take actions to improve the adequacy of people in these positions and to give them the resources and support they need to do their jobs.

- Promotion to supervisory positions should be based on managerial and supervisory competence, rather than on other criteria that are typically used but that are not necessarily related to performance.

- Training in the fundamentals of administration and supervision should be provided to newly promoted middle managers.

- Supervisors should not be given the bargaining rights enjoyed by their subordinates.

PERFORMANCE AND SATISFACTION
IN THE WORKPLACE

To say that managers should be given the authority to manage and held accountable for results is not to say *how* they should manage. Management styles vary, as they should, according to the manager, the nature of the operation, and the people employed to do the job. Yet, whatever the style or approach to management, the general formula for high performance remains the same: capable employees who are motivated in the cooperative pursuit of common objectives.

Financial Compensation

Attracting and keeping capable public employees require adequate compensation. But rising government outlays for wages and benefits have become a major economic and political issue. Attention to several key aspects of compensation policy is required to balance the need for fair and competitive compensation with the fiscal limits of government:

● Although we support the principle of comparability of compensation between the public and private sectors, we believe it should be applied to total compensation, including both tangible and intangible benefits (such as job security and continuity). Comparability should also take into account variations in jobs and conditions of work and in economic and political differences among jurisdictions.

● Total costs of employee benefits should be calculated for both current and future years in estimating compensation costs to government.

● State governments should examine the pension systems of their local governments to assure their actuarial soundness.

Nonfinancial Factors

Adequate compensation may be necessary to attract and keep qualified employees, but it will not guarantee either employee satisfaction or high performance. Given reasonable levels of income, job security, and working conditions, the relative importance of other motivators increases. These values include recognition, responsibility, a sense of achievement, and personal development. A major task of management is to blend the diverse and changing goals of individual employees with the broader purposes of the organization.

There are no new magic formulas for dealing with the shifting and highly diverse values of the work force. However, slavish conformance to old principles of personnel management can prove just as abrasive and wasteful as the eager embrace of the latest human relations fads. We believe that there is great opportunity for evolution and experimentation in the organization and management of people to accomplish public goals while improving the quality of working life. In seeking more effective approaches, managers should consider the following factors:

● Whatever the style of management or work organization, there is need for a clear articulation of goals and objectives and for methods of performance evaluation. The ultimate test of any management approach is results.

● Employees themselves are a prime and important source of knowledge and energy for improving operations. They should be involved in the improvement process both informally and through such mechanisms as labor-management committees.

● In many public-service operations, there is room for experimentation with new forms of work organization that can improve both productivity and the quality of working life. These forms include flexible working hours, creative job design, and greater responsibility for individual employees and groups of employees.

● Greater employee participation should not be confused with the collective bargaining process, which should deal strictly with the terms of employment, not with the nature of public-service operations.

● Vocational, educational, career, and personal interests should be viewed in an integrated manner, not as fragments to be dealt with in isolation from one another.

LEADERSHIP AND NEW PERSPECTIVE

Although the responsibility for providing effective and efficient government lies principally with political leaders and professional managers, these men and women cannot do the job alone. They need the skills, the energies, the imagination, and the cooperation of all public employees and their unions and associations. In turn, all government employees need the support of the public they serve, including business, universities, community groups, and individual citizens. Improving the performance of government requires that elected officials, managers, and employees at all levels of government develop an attitude born of mutual respect for one another, conscious recognition of common goals, and acknowledgment of their joint responsibility and the public trust in which they all are held.

Such cooperative action depends upon the creation of a practical framework for labor relations and personnel management. That framework must deal realistically with the economic and political contexts in which government operates and must provide for the integration of the key components of personnel management: civil service and personnel support functions, collective bargaining, management and supervisory practices, and means of achieving higher performance and satisfaction in work.

Recognizing Diversity

In suggesting a framework for public personnel management, we are conscious of the diversity among the nation's states and localities in size, in services performed, in labor organization, in political and economic circumstances, and in traditions of labor relations and personnel management. Some jurisdictions have traditions of strong merit systems and highly professional management; others have experience with neither. Some have long histories of active trade unions and collective bargaining; others have no experience whatsoever with formal labor relations. Prescriptions for change or improvement must be adapted to local circumstances, and in the end, each state or locality must tailor a set of policies and practices to fit its own unique conditions. Nevertheless, we believe that there is sufficient commonality of experience and that the need to strengthen the public sector at all levels is sufficiently urgent for the guidelines presented in this statement to prove useful to many of the nation's state and local governments if suitably adapted to meet local needs and resources.

Chapter 2

THE POLITICAL ECONOMY OF PUBLIC EMPLOYMENT

PERSONNEL MANAGEMENT IN STATE AND LOCAL GOVERNMENT cannot be divorced from its broader economic and political environment. Over the past twenty years, governments increased wages and benefits in order to compete in the labor market for the number and quality of employees required to provide expanding public services. The growth in the number of public employees resulted in their developing substantial political strength. By organizing their growing ranks and engaging in effective political action, some public employees were able to push for higher wages and benefits. Rising government budgets and taxes resulting from all these factors, as well as concern over performance and labor unrest, have provoked a reaction from taxpayers. The result in many jurisdictions has been growing tension between public employees and taxpayers.

TRENDS IN PUBLIC EMPLOYMENT

From 1955 to 1976, state and local government employment grew at an average annual rate of 4.8 percent, reaching 9,514,463 full-time and 2,654,727 part-time employees in 1976. States and localities now employ more than four times as many people as the federal government and account for 1 in 7 nonagricultural workers in the United States. This expansion in employment coincided with the growth in budgets and programs. (In contrast, during the same period, the federal government's budget grew substantially, but its employment remained reasonably stable.) State and local purchases of goods and services increased from 8.4 percent of GNP in 1957 to 13.2 percent in 1977. In the early 1970s, that rate of growth slowed; and in 1977, it increased only 1.1 percent in real terms, the smallest annual increase since 1951.[1] This slowdown reflected a combination of declines and slower growth in the demand for some public services, especially primary and secondary education. It also reflected the fact that the growth of state and local revenues also slowed in response to the economic recession of the early to mid-1970s. Although the state-local sector will continue to grow, it is unlikely in the near future to experience the rapid growth characteristic of the 1950s and 1960s. In some services, employment levels may actually decline. Nevertheless, the magnitude of employment already attained and the importance of the services provided are themselves significant.

About 73 percent of state and local employees work for local governments (counties, municipalities, townships, school districts, and special districts); the remaining 27 percent work for state governments (see Figure 3). Nearly half the state-local work force is employed in primary, secondary, and higher education (see Appendix B); 80 percent of those in education are employed by independent or semi-independent school districts. Thus, education stands apart not only because of its high proportions of expenditure and employment but also because many school boards are elected, levy their own taxes, and consequently constitute separate political-administrative systems with their own characteristics. The economic, political, and employment problems in education are all the more complex because the number of graduates qualified to teach has continued to grow despite the fact that declining student enrollments have required layoffs of teachers.

The nature of the public work force has been changing along with the nature of the American work force as a whole. Educational levels have increased; larger numbers of women and young people have sought and found gainful employment; consciousness regarding racial and sex-

---

1. *Economic Report of the President* (Washington, D.C.: U.S. Government Printing Office, January 1978).

ual discrimination in employment has been heightened; widespread experience with severe economic deprivation is more remote; the desire for job satisfaction has risen; and the willingness to accept traditional concepts of authority and efficiency has declined. Of course, the magnitude of these changes varies from place to place and among age and educational groups. Nevertheless, their overall impact should not be underestimated. Managers are finding it necessary to rethink traditional notions of supervision and administration.

The state-local government work force has also been rapidly organizing. Between 1968 and 1976, membership in unions and employee associations nearly doubled, from 2.5 million to 4.7 million, or 49.8 percent of full-time workers.[2] (See Figure 4 and Appendix C.) The most highly organized professions are teaching and fire fighting, with 69 percent and 72 percent of full-time employees, respectively, belonging to unions or associations.[3] Teachers also represent the largest occupational group of organized public employees; in 1974, the National Education Association had a membership of 1,470,000, and the American Federation of Teachers had a membership of 444,000.[4] (In contrast, approximately 28.3 percent of all workers in nonagricultural establishments belonged to labor organizations in 1976.)[5]

Unionization has brought collective bargaining to government. By 1976, there were bargaining units in 41 state governments and 9,064 local governments, covering a total of 4,353,589 employees, or 46 percent of the full-time state-local work force.[6] Most big-city governments now bargain formally with their employees, although there are impor-

2. U.S. Bureau of the Census, *Labor-Management Relations in State and Local Governments: 1976*, State and Local Government Special Studies no. 88 (Washington, D.C.: U.S. Government Printing Office, 1978), p. 1.

3. *Labor-Management Relations in State and Local Governments: 1976*, p. 1.

4. U.S. Department of Labor, Bureau of Labor Statistics, *Directory of National Unions and Employee Associations, 1975* (Washington, D.C.: U.S. Government Printing Office, 1977), p. 65.

5. U.S. Department of Labor, Bureau of Labor Statistics, "Labor Union and Employee Association Membership, 1976," *News* (Washington, D.C., 1977). The number of organized employees in the private sector increased from 22.0 million in 1968 to 24.4 million in 1974 and actually dropped slightly to 24.0 million in 1976. The proportion of government workers in all labor organizations in the United States increased from 17.5 percent in 1968 to 22.1 percent in 1974. Because the number of federal workers in labor organizations actually declined during those years (from 1.4 million to 1.3 million), these statistics reflect the growth in state and local unionization. *Directory of National Unions and Employee Associations, 1975*, p. 70.

6. *Labor-Management Relations in State and Local Governments: 1976*, pp. 33, 151.

Figure 3: State and Local Government Employment,
by Type of Government, October 1976

Function	Employees (Full time and Part time)	
	Number (thousands)	Percent
Total	12,169	100.0
State	3,343	27.5
Local	8,826	72.5
County	1,600	13.1
Municipal	2,442	20.1
Township	401	3.3
School districts	3,985	32.5
Special districts	398	3.3

Source: U.S. Department of Commerce, Bureau of the Census, *Public Employment in 1976* (Washington, D.C.: U.S. Government Printing Office, 1977), p. 3.

tant exceptions, such as Chicago. Twenty-eight states have statutes providing for collective bargaining, six prohibit it, and three provide for meet-and-confer relationships. Among those states and localities that do bargain collectively, the laws, procedures, and traditions vary widely.

POLITICAL STRENGTH OF PUBLIC EMPLOYEES

The political influence of state and local government employees has risen principally because their numbers have increased and they consequently represent a larger share of the electorate. Many public-employee groups have capitalized on their numbers through effective organization and political action to influence votes and lobby for legislation. In some jurisdictions, public employees, particularly teachers, are considered the most influential lobby group. Their political strength has been enhanced through collective bargaining and the threat or execution of strikes, slowdowns, or other job actions. Residency requirements (i.e., laws that require employees to live in the jurisdictions in which they work) tend to increase overall public-employee voting strength but also make resident employees confront the inconveniences that result from job actions.

Like jobholders in the private sector, public employees represent a wide cross section of trades and professions, including teachers, police officers, fire fighters, social workers, medical specialists, sanitation workers, and technicians, each with its own traditions and standards. Like private-sector employees, most government workers have a primary interest in their individual jobs and careers that is quite separate from their identification with their occupational group and their identification as government workers.

Like all taxpayers, public employees have an interest in holding down the cost of government. For example, perhaps as many as 45 percent of public employees in California are estimated to have voted for Proposition 13 despite threats of government layoffs. However, interest in lower taxes tends to be at odds with the desire of public employees for higher wages and benefits. They stand to gain more in wage increases than they will have to pay in taxes because the burden of supporting those higher salaries will be spread among all taxpayers. The issue is further complicated by the internal diversity of the state-local work force. Sanitation workers may support higher wages for bus drivers as a way of justifying a future wage increase for themselves, but they must also realize that increased wages for bus drivers will cost them higher taxes or bus fares. Teachers may resent higher relative wages for sanitation workers not only as an unwelcome addition to their tax bill but also as what they perceive to be an inequitable distribution of income.

As recipients of public services, public employees have the same interest in the quality of government as the public at large has. But here again, their interests are far from uniform. Public works personnel may support a teachers' strike in principle as a legitimate way for public employees to apply pressure for higher wages, but they must then accept an educational loss to their children and arrange for baby-sitters or other supervision for the children for the duration of the strike. The limits to solidarity among public employees as a class were reflected in 1975 in San Francisco when most nonuniformed city workers crossed the picket lines of police and fire fighters to get to their jobs.

Figure 4: State and Local Government Organized Employees, by Function, October 1976 (thousands)

Function	Number of Full-Time Employees	Percent of All Full-Time Employees per Function	Number of Organized Full-Time Employees	Percent of All Organized Full-Time Employees per Function
Total	9,514	100.0	4,737	49.8
Education	4,527	47.6	2,637	58.3
Highways	542	5.7	240	44.3
Public welfare	335	3.5	138	41.3
Hospitals	910	9.6	360	39.5
Police protection	531	5.6	288	54.3
Fire protection	210	2.2	151	71.6
Sanitation other than sewerage	119	1.2	59	49.2
All other functions	2,341	24.6	864	36.9

Source: U.S. Bureau of the Census, *Labor-Management Relations in State and Local Governments: 1976*, State and Local Government Special Studies no. 88 (Washington, D.C.: U.S. Government Printing Office, 1978), p. 9.

Public employees share the concern felt by the public at large for community health, safety, and welfare. Many are disturbed by the hostility that seems to characterize public labor relations. Some fear that association with trade unions will taint their status as professionals. At the same time, they feel harassed by incompetent administrators and an uncaring public, they are fearful that they will be unable to keep up with the rising cost of living, and they are very much aware that other groups in American society aggressively pursue their own self-interests through political channels. Consequently, many conclude that they must similarly compete as a group in order to protect their interest in fair compensation and their ability to do their jobs properly.

Diversity of Employee Organizations

The diversity among public employees is reflected in their organizations. There are numerous local craft unions and associations, some fully independent, others affiliated with national labor unions or associations. The American Federation of State, County and Municipal Employees (AFSCME), one of the largest public-employee unions, with approximately 1 million members, is affiliated with the AFL-CIO. AFSCME and other employee groups, including the National Education Association, formed a separate organization called the Coalition of American Public Employees. AFSCME has since withdrawn from the Public Employee Department of the AFL-CIO. Other local or state employee associations join in national coalitions, such as the Assembly of Government Employees. Furthermore, although most organized state and local workers belong to unions or associations made up exclusively of public employees, some have joined unions whose major base of membership is in the private sector, primarily the International Brotherhood of Teamsters, the Service Employees International Union, and the Laborers International Union.

The distinctions among traditional trade unions, employee associations, and professional associations have faded in recent years. For example, the National Education Association, whose membership once encompassed school administrators at all levels, has tended to narrow its focus to nonmanagement personnel; principals, superintendents, and state education officials have gravitated toward separate organizations. The merger of the New York State Civil Service Employees Association with AFSCME in 1978 is a further reflection of the blurred distinction between trade unions and employee associations.

There is intense competition among labor organizations to enlist new members in government. The diversity and rivalry within the public labor movement is generally unrecognized by the public; significantly, it does not seem to be much better understood by elected officials and some government managers. Thus, the turbulence experienced in some jurisdictions in adjusting to the unionization of public employees can be accounted for in part by the tendencies to perceive public unions as a monolithic and cohesive force generally to be feared, to ignore the important ideological differences and organizational rivalries among unions, and to fail to recognize the potential of employee organization to promote labor peace and more effective management. Government officials who fail to recognize the complex political forces at play within and among unions may unwittingly and unnecessarily create conflict.

Like any leader, a union leader's latitude for action depends primarily on his or her standing with the membership and its internal politics. Yet, union leaders typically confront public suspicion, increasingly confident and resistant management, intense competition from rival unions, and diversity of interests among their own members. Older workers tend to favor bargaining for higher pensions; whereas younger workers push for higher salaries. Some members counsel restraint; others press for more militant action.

National labor leaders need to take into account the diversity of circumstances encountered by their locals. The tough rhetoric that may be effective in the fight for recognition in one jurisdiction may be resented and may provoke adverse public reaction in jurisdictions in which unions already enjoy substantial strength. Similarly, when bargaining at the state or local level, public managers should be more attuned to the national goals of employee associations.

PUBLIC ATTITUDES AND POLITICAL CHARACTER

In no jurisdiction do public employees constitute a political force stronger than the combined political strength of the public at large. In some cities, public employees have been able to exercise political influence disproportionate to their relatively small numbers because they were unified, well organized, or well financed or because they enjoyed substantial public sympathy or acquiescence. In New York City, the number of municipal employees is greater than the winning margin of votes for any mayoral election in this century; consequently, a unified bloc of public employees and their supporters could exercise a decisive influence in city elections. However, recent municipal elections in several large cities have demonstrated not only the limited electoral power of public employees but also the potential appeal of politicians who actively campaign against increased government wages and benefits.

Elaborate structures for labor relations and personnel management are no substitute for public officials who are able to deal with the political and managerial complexities of contemporary labor relations. Restrictions on the political activities of public employees such as the so-called Little Hatch Acts may be justifiable as much to protect employees themselves from political pressure imposed by their superiors as to limit employees' participation in partisan politics. But where such restrictions are established, every effort should be made to permit public employees the same *individual* political rights enjoyed by other citizens. This distinction between collective and individual political participation is consistent with the nonpartisan character of the public service. Rather than depend on political restrictions on public employees, the public should rely first on its own political strength to elect officials who will exercise an appropriate balance of concern for the overriding public interest and the rights and interests of public employees.

The public must also recognize that the nature of government and of public employees has changed. There is no evidence to suggest that public workers are distinguishable from their counterparts in the private sector in ability, ambition, educational preparation, range of skills, desire for just compensation, or attitude toward work. The persistence of negative attitudes toward public employees expressed in the media or by business people, politicians, and the general public perpetuates bad feelings, complicates personnel problems, and poses a challenge to the enterprise of public officials and the dedication of employees.

DISTINCTIONS BETWEEN
PUBLIC AND PRIVATE LABOR RELATIONS

Private-sector labor relations practices cannot be wholly transplanted to the public sector because of several important distinctive characteristics of government.

First, public employees participate in the selection of their employers (i.e., elected officials) by voting for or supporting candidates for public office. Office seekers are thus sensitive to a political constituency that is concerned with the wages, hours, and working conditions of public jobs. Employee organizations also lobby public officials to influence public policy in their favor; the success of their lobbying is, of course, related to their political influence on elections.

Second, whereas job actions such as strikes or work slowdowns in the private sector are usually designed to inflict economic hardship on the employer to force a favorable settlement, job actions in the public sector are designed to apply political pressure to public officials to settle on terms favorable to employees. But job actions by some public employees may curtail or eliminate critical public services and thus could endanger life or cause irreparable injury to individual citizens or the community as a whole. The failure of public employees to perform essential services, for whatever reason, can leave the public without the means of ensuring that these basic needs are met.

This is not to suggest that all public services are of equal importance simply because they are public. Some government operations are no more essential to protecting community health, safety, and welfare than many private enterprises are. Conversely, some private activities, such as the delivery of heating fuel in winter, can be just as essential to health as certain government services. The relative importance of a service depends, not upon whether it is public or private, but upon whether its cessation will jeopardize the health, safety, or welfare of the community.

Government has a fundamental responsibility to protect life and property, maintain order, and assure justice, and it enjoys monopoly status in meeting that responsibility. Government's special role as the ultimate guardian of the public requires that it be able to take action to protect the public interest in the event that essential services are threatened, whether those services are public or private.

Third, whereas competition and market forces generally provide incentives to keep costs down and promote effective operations in business, political pressure is the principal disciplinary force in government. Business revenue derives from the sale of a specific product or service, but government revenue is generated principally through general taxes that are distantly and ambiguously related to the value of services performed. Taxpayers may register their general dissatisfaction with the overall quality or cost of government by moving, by voting against candidates perceived as inefficient or ineffectual, or by opposing referenda on bonds or tax rate increases. But to the extent that market discipline exists in the public sector, it is cumbersome, slow, and imprecise. As a consequence, although unions in the private sector are likely at some point to consider the impact of their demands on the competitiveness of their employers and thus on their own job security and other interests, public employees may be more inclined to push for higher wages, believing that their government can generate new revenue by increasing taxes or securing state or federal grants.

There are, of course, exceptions to these propositions. Oligopolistic businesses enjoy greater control over prices than businesses in competitive markets and thus can more easily pass on higher employee costs in the form of higher prices without great risk to revenues. And some public unions have recognized that excessive wage gains can drive out taxpayers and undermine the tax base on which they depend for future jobs and compensation. As public resistance to higher taxes increases, politicians find greater political support for holding down public employees' wages.

ECONOMIC AND FISCAL CONSTRAINTS

The ability of a local government to pay employee compensation is dependent on the tax base, taxing authority, the willingness of the public to be taxed, prevailing national and regional economic conditions, intergovernmental fiscal policy, and the jurisdiction's borrowing capacity. Local governments have little or no control over general economic conditions or intergovernmental fiscal policy. Their revenues are tied in some measure to cycles of economic growth and decline and to changing national and regional patterns of economic activity and residential location. The standards and programs mandated by higher levels of government directly affect local expenditures, just as grants and state-allowed taxing authority affect local revenues.

Local governments do have some control over the nature of the local economy through policies regarding tax levels, land use and other regulation, and the quality of public services, policies that may attract or repel businesses and residents. Recruiting larger numbers of employees with greater skills or capabilities in order to provide more and/or better public services requires a larger tax burden. Weighing such considerations and their effects on local economic health is a task best left as much as possible to the community itself, which will enjoy the benefits of wise decisions and shoulder the costs of poor decisions. However, the flexibility of local governments to make such decisions is increasingly constrained by limited revenue sources. In most states, local authority to raise revenues through sales and income taxes is strictly limited or prohibited altogether. Such measures as California's Proposition 13 aim to restrict the only other major source of local revenue, the property tax. Under such constraints, many local governments will quickly reach the limits of their ability to raise revenues and thereby become increasingly dependent on state and federal financing. One result will be a limit on their ability to make trade-offs regarding tax rates, employee compensation, quality of public services, and the effects of these decisions on the ability to attract or retain businesses and residents. Should this trend continue, such issues and choices, including wages and benefits of local government employees, will be increasingly resolved or predominantly influenced at the state level.

It can be difficult to disentangle those economic and fiscal factors over which a local government has substantial control from those over which it has little or no control. For example, a city government with disproportionately high welfare burdens will have less money to pay for wages and benefits for public employees. However, when fiscal difficulties result from a city government's own mismanagement or profligacy, officials may claim that their inability to finance higher public wages and benefits is due to the burdens of programs mandated by state and federal government. The ability of a local government to pay employee compensation that is both fair and adequate to recruit and retain needed workers and to avoid labor unrest cannot be disassociated from intergovernmental economic and fiscal policy.

IMPLICATIONS
FOR PERSONNEL MANAGEMENT

A dynamic operates among the economic, political, and managerial factors that affect public service and its employees. The demand for public services is politically determined; yet, the judgment of elected officials and voters concerning adequate levels of services is heavily conditioned by the cost of those services. Cost, in turn, is determined partly by market forces that govern the price of goods and labor and partly by the political influence of public employees. That political influence is exercised partly through support of sympathetic candidates and through lobbying and partly through the threat to withhold public services through strikes or job actions. Labor disruption, in turn, is a managerial problem with strong political ramifications; strikes might cause citizens to demand costly settlements that will increase taxes, or they might anger voters into supporting public officials committed to restraining future wage increases for government workers.

The situation is further complicated by the fact that public employees are only one of many groups competing politically for public funds. Citizens lobby for services and direct cash transfers. Taxpayers fight to restrain expenditures. Businesses seek services and tax breaks and also argue for restraint in government spending. The entanglement of that political competition with more traditional economic concerns is burdening government decision making in all areas, including labor relations.

When elected officials are unable to reconcile those competing political interests in order to forge a common and cohesive policy, government agencies and the managers and employees who make up those agencies are left without clear direction. In the absence of clear goals, agency personnel may do nothing out of fear of criticism or simple inertia, or they may take action based on their own perceptions of public need or their own self-interest. Those actions will be influenced in part by the same interest groups that lobby elected officials and that do not hesitate to lobby government agencies directly if those agencies make the key decisions. In such circumstances, public employees have an edge over other lobby groups for the simple reason that they constitute the personnel of government agencies.

Consequently, problems that are frequently associated with government workers, such as ineffectual programs, wasteful spending, and misguided government action, are in fact likely to derive from the political fragmentation characteristic of so many state and local jurisdictions. To the extent that various public employees themselves constitute some of the many political groups that aggressively pursue their own self-interests with insufficient regard for the broader public interest, they must share the responsibility. But the many other political groups that lobby government in the same manner must also share the responsibility for public policy and government operations that are confused, contradictory, and wasteful.

The fact is that because political power in many states, cities, and counties is highly diffused, forging more coherent public policy will depend upon the extent to which numerous competing groups, including public employees, can reach accord or form more stable coalitions capable of governing effectively and fairly.

The structure of personnel management in state and local government must take all these factors into account. Because economic, political, and government characteristics vary widely from state to state and from community to community, it is not possible to design a model personnel system that will serve equally well in every jurisdiction. Responsibility for establishing effective structures rests principally with each state and local jurisdiction, where the political forces and economic constraints can best be balanced to provide stability and fairness in managing the public work force.

Chapter 3

A STRUCTURE FOR PERSONNEL MANAGEMENT

POLITICAL CONSIDERATIONS have long affected public employment and personnel management. In the nineteenth century, state and local governments hired and fired people largely on the basis of patronage. Toward the end of the century, coalitions slowly began to form to replace the patronage system with civil service or merit systems under which government employees were hired on the basis of their ability to perform as determined by competitive examinations and were granted protection from political abuse and arbitrary firing. The coalition pushing for merit systems included government workers who sought job security and checks against political pressure applied by superiors and civic groups that sought to improve the efficiency of government by hiring qualified people and to curb the corruption and political abuses that tend to be associated with patronage.

The impetus for reform came at the local level. In 1877, the New York Civil Service Reform Association was created to push for the elimination of patronage and the establishment of merit principles for the public service in New York City, New York State, and the federal government. Similar organizations were soon formed in other cities, and in 1881, they merged, creating the National Civil Service Reform League (the forerunner of the present National Civil Service League).[1] It was this movement that formulated and lobbied for the passage of the Pendleton Act of 1883, which established the federal civil service system.

In 1883, New York State also passed a civil service law that applied to county and city as well as state employees. Massachusetts followed suit in 1884. Several big cities subsequently passed their own civil service laws. Yet, by 1934, only eight states had passed such laws; and of those, the Connecticut law was eventually repealed, and the Kansas law remained dormant because the legislature refused to appropriate funds for its enforcement.

In 1939, the federal government gave new impetus to the adoption of merit standards in state governments by requiring that state employees administering Social Security Board programs be covered by a merit system. In 1970, Congress passed the Intergovernmental Personnel Act (IPA) to improve the quality of public service through technical and financial assistance, talent sharing, training, and the promotion of merit principles in state and local government personnel systems. The IPA program, administered by the U.S. Civil Service Commission, has been instrumental in developing a broader perspective on public personnel management and encouraging experimentation with means of improving the public service at the state and local levels.

Thirty-five states now have central personnel agencies employing merit standards generally in conformance with IPA principles. Twenty-eight of those states have recruitment programs that attempt to reach a broad spectrum of the population, award entry positions on the basis of open competition, and hold competitive examinations for promotion to higher positions.[2] The other fifteen states have more limited merit systems that cover employees in some federally funded programs. Virtually every major city and most cities with a population of more than 100,000 have adopted formal merit systems covering most of their employees, although many smaller cities have not.

---

1. In 1970, the National Civil Service League published a model public personnel administration law advocating the reform of traditional merit systems, of which the league was an early and persistent supporter, to reverse what it believed to be antimerit tendencies that had crept into civil service practice over the years.

2. U.S. Civil Service Commission, Bureau of Intergovernmental Personnel Programs, *Statistical Report on State Personnel Operations* (Washington, D.C., January 1977).

The civil service reform movement occurred as governments in the larger states and cities were developing into large, technical, and increasingly bureaucratic organizations. The political pressure for greater emphasis on merit reinforced the otherwise natural need for the larger organizations to delegate certain tasks of personnel management to specialists, including recruiting, selecting, classifying, and setting pay levels. These tasks and the personnel specialists who administered them tended to be grouped into centralized departments of personnel administration. The more technical the tasks of government became, the greater the requirement to hire people with adequate skills. Thus, the evolving complexity of government to some extent created its own pressure to impose merit standards on itself. In the jurisdictions that adopted merit systems, the bureaucratic necessity for more specialized personnel administration became intertwined with the goals and purpose of the merit system, which generally was entrusted to an independent civil service board. And even those governments without formal merit or civil service systems have nonetheless developed similar specialized departments of personnel administration with formal regulations, procedures, and personnel specialists.

DEFICIENCIES IN MERIT SYSTEMS
AND PERSONNEL ADMINISTRATION

For several years now, there has been a growing awareness that many merit systems do not function according to merit principles. Because these systems were conceived primarily as mechanisms for checking abuses, they tend to be geared more to preventing negative behavior than to promoting positive behavior. Greater emphasis is placed on protecting against abuse of authority than on permitting top managers the authority they need to improve performance.

The specialization and bureaucratization of personnel administration has created related problems. Although personnel departments are responsible only for selected aspects of overall personnel management, public managers and personnel specialists often equate the limited support function of personnel administration with the broader responsibility for personnel management. Housed as they are in a separate department, the support functions tend to take on an importance of their own that may become detached from the goal of improving government performance. Managers seeking better performance complain that restrictive personnel practices impede their efforts; managers looking for excuses tend to hide behind them. These tendencies are reinforced by the inclination of some personnel departments to promote such bureaucratic self-interests as expansion, protection of turf, and professional preoccupation with technique that may have little to do with developing and using employee capability.

A number of deficiencies are commonly cited:

● *Recruitment Is Slow, Unimaginative, and Unaggressive.* Whereas private companies (and many federal agencies) actively seek out and woo top talent, many state and local personnel offices, often mired in red tape and a passive, bureaucratic tradition, tend to accept whoever is attracted by general recruitment announcements. In recent years, some states and cities have mounted effective recruitment campaigns, but even these have been cut back in the face of increasing fiscal pressure.

● *Selection Procedures Inhibit the Hiring of the Most Qualified People.* Managers are forced to pick the top scorer or from among the three to five top scorers on written examinations. It is typical for qualified candidates to be distinguished from nonqualified candidates by a difference of one-tenth of a percentage point in scores on examinations that may bear little relation to ability in the first place.

● *Job Vacancies Go Unfilled.* Bureaucratic delays prevent managers from maintaining the work force at full strength, slow the work process, require paying unnecessary overtime, and force the hiring of unqualified people on a temporary basis. Jurisdictions are sometimes so slow that by the time they fill vacancies, the highest-caliber applicants have taken jobs elsewhere.[3]

● *Rigid Classification Systems Impede Efficient Assignment of Work.* The work of overburdened employees cannot be shifted to those who are underutilized. The flexibility for meeting changing conditions and objectives is lost. This is a particularly serious problem for those cities facing reductions in employment levels.

---

3. E. S. Savas and Sigmund S. Ginsburg, "The Civil Service: A Meritless System?" *The Public Interest* 32 (Summer 1973).

● *Promotion and Salary Increases Are Based Largely on Criteria Unrelated to Future Performance.* Excessive reliance on written examinations, seniority, or other factors that have little or no correlation with performance in the new job limits the use of talent, hinders overall agency performance, and causes resentment and frustration among capable employees. The problem lies not just in employees' reluctance to be evaluated but also in supervisors' aversion to giving negative performance assessments.

● *Managers and Supervisors Lack Authority to Reward Superior Performance and Discipline or Fire Nonperformers.* Attempts to fire reputedly flagrant nonperformers are frustrated by unduly lengthy appeals procedures or by reinstatement by civil service boards or courts. Managers learn to work around nonperformers rather than spend the time necessary to have them transferred or terminated. Superior performance often goes unrewarded. And the emphasis on objective criteria to gauge performance gives rise to charges of favoritism if managers do reward or promote people whose talents are not readily measurable by objective criteria.

● *The Merit Principle Is Further Diluted by Other Public Goals.* Laws requiring preference in selection for government jobs to be given to veterans may be politically or socially desirable, but they can be at odds with selection strictly on the basis of merit. Affirmative action to eliminate discrimination in hiring and promotion can support the merit principle by opening jobs to all qualified applicants, but de facto quotas for various groups can impede the hiring of people on the basis of capability alone. The issue of appropriate criteria for selection for government jobs is complex not only because government traditionally has been a route to employment for those who may have been economically disadvantaged but who have achieved a measure of political power but also because it is argued that qualifications or ability to perform may in fact depend upon such factors as racial representativeness (e.g., black police officers, some argue, may be more effective in black neighborhoods than white police officers) as well as more conventional merit criteria (e.g., education, experience, training, and knowledge).

One recent study of the impact of personnel management on the productivity of city government concluded that "performance [of employees and managers] does not appear to be the central theme of many established systems of personnel management."[4] The eight-city survey indicated that the areas of personnel management which present the greatest impediments to productivity are classification, compensation, selection and promotion, and collective bargaining; those found most supportive are performance appraisal, employee development, and employee-employer relations (see Figure 5).

The sheer growth in the size of government has been at the root of many of the problems associated with public personnel management. The greater the number of employees and the more advanced and specialized the jobs they perform, the more complex the tasks of recruitment, selection, classification, and compensation become. More demanding standards of fairness have created added burdens for the personnel profession: affirmative action to assure recruitment of disadvantaged groups, competitive examinations that are culturally fair and clearly related to the jobs, increased sensitivity to protection against political abuse, and the power of employees to demand protective mechanisms. These and other concerns have been reflected in federal laws that have created new responsibilities and complexities for state and local personnel systems: the Age Discrimination and Employment Act (1967), the Equal Pay Act (1963), the Fair Labor Standards Act (1938), the Equal Employment Opportunity Act (1972), and the Occupational Safety and Health Act (1970). In addition to taxing the technical capability of personnel professionals, these new requirements have significantly increased litigation in public personnel matters.

State and local personnel policy has also been affected by the use of government to create jobs for the unemployed. The primary purpose of the Comprehensive Employment and Training Act (CETA), which Congress passed in 1973, is to provide jobs for the chronically hard-to-employ.[5] The CETA program is administered by state and local government agencies with federal supervision and relies extensively on government agencies to create new jobs. Problems have arisen. In some instances, CETA employees have been hired in agencies that were

---

4. Selma J. Mushkin and Frank H. Sandifer, "Personnel Management and Productivity in City Government" (Washington, D.C.: Public Services Laboratory, Georgetown University, March 1978), p. 144.

5. See *Jobs for the Hard-to-Employ: New Directions for a Public-Private Partnership* (January 1978).

simultaneously laying off regular staff to reduce costs. In other cases, CETA funds have been used to avert layoffs of regular government employees, thereby relieving pressure for staff reductions and diverting federal funds from their intended purpose of providing jobs for the hard-to-employ.

The changing nature and increasingly diverse attitudes of the work force have also challenged accepted ideas and practices related to training and supervision. And rising public concern over the cost and performance of government has exerted added pressure for documented standards of accomplishment and evaluation of results.

Responding to these changes presents a singularly formidable challenge. It has been further complicated by collective bargaining.

IMPACT OF COLLECTIVE BARGAINING

One noted expert has called labor relations "the greatest personnel 'add-on' of all times . . . a development since the 1950s that threatens or promises (depending on one's viewpoint) to reverse which function is the add-on and then to become the central thrust of public personnel administration."[6]

There can be no question that collective bargaining affects key aspects of traditional personnel systems. However, the extent of its impact varies according to specific provisions of laws governing personnel matters and according to positions taken in negotiations by government employers and employees. It is not likely that collective bargaining will fully supplant traditional personnel systems. Nevertheless, special care is required if the two are to work in harmony.

In collective bargaining, employees participate in determining terms and conditions of employment formerly established unilaterally by government through legislation, decisions of civil service boards, or promulgation of directives by personnel departments. Collective bargaining usually covers items that have traditionally been within the purview of merit systems or personnel administration: financial compensation, grievance procedures, and promotion policy. Other traditional

---

6. Chester A. Newland, "Public Personnel Administration: Legalistic Reforms Vs. Effectiveness, Efficiency, and Economy," *Public Administration Review*, no. 5 (September-October 1976), p. 532.

Figure 5: Personnel Practices That Impede Productivity (percent)

Procedures for getting positions classified properly	Impede	No impact	Help
	45.9	17.3	36.8
Procedures for establishing or changing pay levels	48.2	18.1	33.7
Policies and procedures for rewarding superior performance (through increased pay or benefits)	43.5	28.7	27.8
Policies and procedures for terminating employees for cause	44.4	27.6	28.0
Procedures for processing promotion, transfer, and termination actions	39.8	29.5	30.6
Number of separate bargaining units (collective bargaining)	52.2	38.9	8.9
Attitude of unions or employee organizations toward productivity as a bargaining issue	60.8	27.8	11.4

Source: Selma J. Mushkin and Frank H. Sandifer, "Personnel Management and Productivity in City Government," (Washington, D.C.: Public Services Laboratory, Georgetown University, March 1978), p. 32.

civil service concerns such as recruitment, selection, job classification, transfer, discipline, and discharge may also be affected by bargaining, depending upon the scope of bargaining defined by state law and the willingness of management or desire of labor to negotiate topics that affect such functions.[7] Formal merit systems and personnel administration will continue to set policy for matters not covered by bargaining, for employees who do not bargain collectively, and in some cases, for the administration of contracts negotiated through collective bargaining.

Concern that collective bargaining might subvert traditional merit systems should be tempered by recognition of the deficiencies in current civil service practice. Some of the potential consequences of collective bargaining that could restrict management are not so different from restrictions management already faces under current civil service practice. For example, some unions favor restrictions on management discretion in hiring and promotion; current personnel practice reflects the same inclinations. Most unions claim to support the merit principle but tend to define merit as a minimum standard of qualification or performance rather than as a relative assessment of capability or accomplishment with an emphasis on excellence; existing civil service regulations have the same bias.

Such overlapping issues can create confusion unless state laws clearly distinguish between the responsibilities of civil service and collective bargaining. States have taken different approaches. Some emphasize the predominance of merit regulations; others emphasize collective bargaining. Some state laws attempt to specify which personnel matters are the responsibility of civil service authority and which should be covered in negotiated contracts, although even in these cases court interpretation may vary on a case-by-case basis. (These issues are treated in greater detail in Chapter 4.)

MODERNIZING PERSONNEL SYSTEMS

The strengthening of state and local personnel systems needs to begin with a clear recognition of the distinctions among personnel

---

7. David T. Stanley, *Managing Local Government Under Union Pressure* (Washington, D.C.: Brookings Institution, 1972), p. 138.

management, the specialized tasks of personnel administration, merit systems, and the role of collective bargaining. Personnel management should have as its broad purpose the promotion of human development in order to achieve the effective use and fair treatment of employees for the efficient and effective accomplishment of organizational objectives. Functions such as recruitment, selection, classification, promotion, and compensation, which are commonly grouped under the heading of personnel administration, are only one set of tasks performed in support of personnel management. Merit systems nominally attempt to apply merit principles (such as those enumerated on page 57) to those functions. Collective bargaining provides employees with a voice in setting the terms of employment, but it should not supplant the traditional function of personnel administration or more than partially affect the means of pursuing the major goal of personnel management. Nor should collective bargaining undermine adherence to merit principles.

Varying Roles of Government Personnel

Public personnel systems need to take into account the roles and relations among all the people employed by government. Modern state and local government is simultaneously a service organization that requires professional management and a political institution with legitimate political tasks to perform. Top policy officials in government are politically selected, as they should be. But they should be able to deal with the managerial complexities of government, and they are increasingly called upon to do so. Professional managers should have the training and experience to assure that the large and complex service operations of government function effectively and efficiently in the pursuit of public objectives, but they must also be sensitive to the legitimate political concerns of elected officials. Other public employees who work in service agencies should be hired for their technical capabilities and skills, and they need to be protected against political abuse. **We recommend that the personnel systems of most state governments and the larger local governments distinguish among top policy makers, professional managers, and other employees.**

The distinctions among these three groups are, of course, less than precise in every instance. Many top policy officials also have major managerial responsibilities, and professional managers may have explicit or de facto policy responsibilities. For example, a mayor or elected county executive is both a policy maker and a manager; a city manager is considered to be a professional, and yet exercises policy judgments and usually serves at the pleasure of a city council, a situation that requires political skill and sensitivity. A professional police chief not only manages but also makes policy explicitly or through interpretation in the course of its implementation. Many employees in line operations are required to use discretion and judgment in interpreting—and therefore determining—government policy. For example, a teacher exercises considerable professional judgment in instructing children within the curriculum guidelines established by school officials. Conversely, many people in formally defined managerial or supervisory positions are engaged more in routine administrative work than in activities that require the exercise of managerial skills and judgment. Yet, despite this blurring of distinctions, the classifications are useful for the purpose of establishing a more flexible personnel structure tailored to the responsibilities of different government positions.

● *Top Policy Personnel.* Governors, mayors, elected county executives, state legislators, city and county council members, and other elected officials are all top policy personnel. So, too, are the top appointed officials of government, especially those who serve at the pleasure of elected officials. The chief executive officer in any government, whether an elected official or a professional manager, should have the authority to appoint to top policy positions people who will serve at his or her pleasure. Such appointees may themselves be professional managers. We are aware of the potential danger of appointments to top positions in government for essentially political purposes and with little regard for ability to perform. Nevertheless, we believe that if officials who are elected by the public or professional chief administrative officers who serve at the pleasure of elected officials are to make government perform in accordance with the public's expectations they must have the authority to hire people who are compatible with their policies and philosophies and who are accountable to them.

Governments should improve the effectiveness with which they use their top policy personnel. Legislative bodies in particular, including state legislatures and city and county councils, often misuse the limited time and energy of their members through too much attention to detail to the exclusion of broader policy considerations or through inadequate staff assistance. Many elected executives and their top policy appointees similarly fail to use their time appropriately. Some governments have found it desirable to provide their elected officials with training in the technical operations of government. Sound public personnel policy should begin at the top with the effective organization and management of the time and talents of top policy makers.

● *Professional Managers.* A second set of personnel policies would apply to professional managers. Although most professional managers are not selected politically, they nonetheless represent the interest of the government in assuring that policy is carried out. On the one hand, they require protection from political whim, which can undermine their professional status and the continuity and effectiveness of government services; on the other hand, they should be responsive to the legitimate interests and desires of top policy makers. Achieving such a balance between political goals and professional standards requires establishing conditions of employment that are more insulated from political volatility than those that apply to top policy officials yet less structured and more flexible than those established for employees below the managerial ranks.

Certain classes of professional, technical, and confidential employees should be similarly treated. The complexity of government requires the proficient and reliable assistance of staff whose loyalty and accountability to top policy makers and managers can be counted on. Flexibility in pay and mobility of assignment can also be important to attract and effectively use scarce staff and other technical talent.

● *Other Public Employees.* The third part of the personnel system would consist of other employees who would be covered by a more formally structured merit system or, for those employees engaging in collective bargaining, an appropriate combination of a merit system and provisions established through bargaining. It is primarily for this group that the suggestions in the remainder of this chapter (and in Chapter 4) are intended.

Executive Responsibility for Personnel Management

The diffusion of responsibility for personnel matters among civil service commissions, personnel boards and departments, and labor relations offices creates unnecessary problems of coordination and even competition among staffs and causes confusion in the formulation and administration of personnel policy. For example, collective bargaining and the administration of labor contracts are integral to other personnel support functions. There may be justification for keeping labor relations activities separate from personnel matters; however, we believe that for most jurisdictions, there are benefits to consolidating the two functions in a single agency, even if they are located in separate divisions within the agency. The policy-making powers of civil service commissions and personnel boards need to be more closely related to other personnel concerns, including labor relations, and hence should also be incorporated in the department dealing with personnel and employee relations. All these functions should be under the control of the chief executive in order to facilitate the integration of personnel management with other aspects of government management. **We recommend the consolidation of the various support functions typically associated with personnel administration, civil service, and labor relations into a single department of personnel or employee relations under the authority and responsibility of the chief executive officer.**

In many governments, it may be desirable to decentralize the personnel support functions so that individual agencies and managers will have flexibility in designing personnel practices in keeping with their particular needs. However, decentralization should be accompanied by government-wide personnel policy that is clearly defined at least in terms of goals and objectives, if not in the details of practices and procedures, to assure consistency and the observance of common standards throughout the government. For most governments, collective bargaining should be centralized, but there should be provision for the involvement of operating managers (see Chapter 5).

Protection of Employees and Merit Principles

If actions are taken to give the chief executive greater authority over personnel matters, steps should be taken simultaneously to assure adequate protection of employees against political abuse and arbitrary action by supervisors. **We recommend the creation of an independent board primarily responsible to the council or legislature and charged with assuring that merit principles are observed in public employment.** The board would be responsible for hearing and deciding grievances and appeals from employees, for investigating suspected violations of merit procedure, and for conducting inquiries and issuing advisory opinions on personnel policies and practices. The board's legislative mandate should clearly indicate that it is to be an appeals and investigatory body responsible for protecting the merit principle, not a policy-making body. Vigilance will be required to assure that the board does not use its appeals and investigatory powers to become a de facto personnel policy-making board in competition with the personnel management system of the executive branch. Provision should also be made for the establishment of separate grievance procedures in those jurisdictions that have collective bargaining.

Revitalizing Merit Principles

It may appear paradoxical that although there is mounting pressure for reform of civil service procedures at the state and local levels, governments that do not have formal merit systems are encouraged to adopt them. Part of the problem may lie in reading too much into the terms *merit* and *civil service*. Personnel systems that do not profess to be merit-oriented may nonetheless place as much (or as little) emphasis on hiring and promoting capable people as formal merit systems that have become encrusted with rigid procedures over the years. Thus, distinguishing among different types of personnel systems on the basis of their labeling may be a pointless exercise. Instead, emphasis should be placed on articulating and pursuing a set of positive principles and practices that assure the highest-quality personnel and the highest-possible performance in government service. **State and local governments, whether or not they have adopted formal merit systems, should examine their personnel policies and practices to assure that they do in fact reflect merit principles in recruitment and selection, job classification, assignment and promotion, discipline and separation, performance appraisal, and equal employment opportunity.**

Government personnel policy needs to move beyond emphasizing minimal standards of performance, guarding against incompetent appointments, and other negative factors and instead place greater emphasis on encouraging excellence, pursuing quality candidates, and removing the impediments that keep managers and employees alike from using their abilities to the fullest. Specific changes are required in several areas:

● *Recruitment and Selection.* Government recruitment programs should more aggressively and imaginatively pursue the best talent available in order to compete with ambitious private-sector recruitment programs. Recruitment programs should be established by or for high schools to inform students of job opportunities and requirements in government. Government agencies should send recruiters to colleges and graduate schools to inform graduating students of the opportunities for rewarding and useful careers or job experiences in state and local government.

Continued efforts are necessary to assure that entrance requirements and examinations are not perfunctory screening devices that bear little relation to work to be performed but rather emphasize the qualities and qualifications needed for high performance in specific government jobs. Restrictive selection procedures, such as the rule of three, should be substantially relaxed so that managers have greater latitude in choosing new employees on the basis of skills and abilities that are required for the work to be performed in their agencies. Lateral entry of employees from other agencies or from outside the government should be facilitated to encourage finding the best person for the job and to assure the infusion of new ideas.

● *Job Classification.* Classifications for jobs should be sufficiently broad to permit employees to use their range of skills and to permit managers flexibility in using staff according to changing work loads and agency objectives. Conventional classification starts with the premise that a given job is necessary and valid to the work of the agency and proceeds to describe the work performed by employees in defining the job's duties, requirements, and ultimately, classification. Modern classification should begin by defining agency goals and should then define the types of jobs or the qualifications of personnel required to perform the work that will lead to the accomplishment of agency objectives. Personnel specialists must understand the objectives and nature of public-service operations and must work more closely with budget and analytic staff in determining personnel needs as they relate to the mission of, and fiscal restraints on, government.

● *Assignment and Promotion.* Flexibility in assignment depends in part on having reasonable job classification standards, but it also requires giving managers greater authority to shift employees to

---

MERIT PRINCIPLES
As enunciated by the Congress in the
Intergovernmental Personnel Act of 1970

1. Recruiting, selecting, and advancing employees on the basis of their relative ability, knowledge, and skills, including open consideration of qualified applicants for initial appointment

2. Providing equitable and adequate compensation

3. Training employees, as needed, to assure high-quality performance

4. Retaining employees on the basis of the adequacy of their performance and separating employees whose inadequate performance cannot be corrected

5. Assuring fair treatment of applicants and employees in all aspects of personnel administration without regard to political affiliation, race, color, national origin, sex, or religious creed and with proper regard for their privacy and constitutional rights as citizens

6. Assuring that employees are protected against coercion for partisan political purposes and are prohibited from using their official authority for the purpose of interfering with or affecting the result of an election or nomination for office

---

where they are needed as tasks, work loads, or agency missions change. Promotion to assignments with greater responsibility should be based on likely ability to perform in the new job as determined through a combination of factors, including supervisor judgment and testing for required skills. Performance in the current job and experience are valid considerations, but neither should be the exclusive criterion for judging fitness for promotion to a job that may require different skills.

● *Discipline and Separation.* Although we stress the importance of personnel management that encourages positive performance and to the greatest extent possible frees both employees and managers from restrictive practices that frustrate productive work, we are nonetheless concerned that current personnel practice makes it difficult to discipline or fire underperformers. In many governments, the problem of terminating employees stems from an endless and complicated appeals process that is often unduly taxing on managers. The consequence is that many managers avoid discipline or firing and attempt to work around unproductive or obstructive employees. Although we recognize the need for an effective and fair appeals process that protects employees from arbitrary action or political manipulation, we believe that employee appeals should in most cases be radically simplified so that the facts of a case can be fairly and fully presented in a single substantive review and the case resolved expeditiously.

● *Performance Appraisal.* Governments periodically experiment with performance appraisal systems, but typically, these soon become perfunctory. Few managers want to antagonize employees with poor ratings, especially when the potential for discipline or firing is limited. However, the greatest deficiency in performance appraisal is the lack of clear measures of agency performance and of individual performance as it is tied to agency objectives. Without clear indicators of agency accomplishment (or of accomplishment within an agency's work units), it is difficult to determine to what extent individual employees are contributing to agency objectives.

Nonetheless, we believe that it is possible to establish more meaningful techniques of evaluating individual performance as it is related to agency objectives and performance indicators and that formal evaluation should weigh more heavily in decisions regarding salary increases, promotions, and job assignments. There are useful measures of agency performance that are not widely applied but that could provide the basis for better program evaluation and, in turn, evaluation of individual performance. Progress has also been made in establishing more meaningful techniques for assessing individual performance that combine quantitative indicators, the use of assessment centers to test for a variety of skills, and informed supervisor judgment.

● *Equal Employment Opportunity.* There should no longer be any doubt about any institution's commitment to eliminating job discrimination on the basis of race, religion, age, sex, national origin, or infirmity that is unrelated to job performance. Hiring, assignment, and promotion should be based exclusively on ability and performance. Nonetheless, social tradition has produced institutional obstacles and attitudes that do in fact discriminate against blacks, women, the very young and very old, the handicapped, and other groups. In a survey of 172 large jurisdictions, the U.S. Civil Service Commission found that one-third of the governments did not prohibit discrimination and that only 42 percent had affirmative action programs.[8]

Specific, aggressive action is required to assure that even the subtlest discriminatory practices are eliminated in hiring, promotion, and compensation policy. Special attention should be given to positions in which groups are underrepresented in order to determine and correct the cause of that underrepresentation. Examinations for selection and placement need to be pruned of biases that may unintentionally discriminate against certain groups. Affirmative action to eliminate job discrimination should not simply be the business of a special program or agency; it should become a conscious component of policy and daily practice at *all* levels of government.

This is not to suggest that employment policy should in any way dilute the merit principle by favoring particular groups. Ability to perform in the job should be the exclusive criterion for public employment, and tendencies to dilute the merit principle for the advantage of any group should be strongly resisted.

● *Planning for Future Staffing Needs.* State and local governments have frequently been caught unprepared to deal with sudden changes in staffing patterns, quantitative changes in staffing levels, and changes in the size, composition, and cost of the labor force.

8. U.S. Civil Service Commission, Bureau of Intergovernmental Personnel Programs, *A Graphic Presentation of Public Personnel Systems in 172 Larger Cities and Counties* (Washington, D.C., September 1976), p. 23.

During the past twenty-five years, many governments have experienced substantial increases in personnel levels as they have worked to produce the growing level of government services demanded by the public. Other governments, especially those in large cities in the Northeast and Midwest, have been faced with the new experience of having to cut back on both service levels and number of employees. In neither case has there been adequate planning that could have anticipated these changes and prepared for them in a way that would have minimized the problems of transition.

Personnel departments should increasingly be held responsible for planning for future staffing patterns by projecting the levels and types of public services that will be required, the numbers and types of personnel that will be needed to carry them out (which will require understanding of changes in public-service technology), the quantity of skills likely to be available in the labor market and the demand that will determine the cost of those skills, and the adequacy of government revenues to cover future staffing needs.

Integrating Personnel Functions with Related Management Concerns

Personnel systems that adopt these general features and functions should be better prepared to handle the growing complexity of modern public personnel management. However, no matter how comprehensive personnel policy and practice attempt to be, they can never be divorced from other components of public management that relate indirectly to personnel matters, and no attempt should be made to do so. There are few aspects of government operation that do not in some way involve or affect employees, and those relationships need to be more consciously taken into account in formulating personnel policy.

Each of the key staff functions has responsibilities that affect public employment. Planning offices should more systematically anticipate changing work force needs related to changing service demands. Budget or finance offices need to forecast future personnel costs related to numbers of employees, wage and benefit levels, and pension obligations and to anticipate the potential of revenues to pay for them. Budget and management offices would benefit from information provided by personnel specialists on the relative importance of specific jobs in meeting program objectives. Legal offices will be increasingly involved in labor litigation. Coordination among these activities is essential to effective personnel policy and is the responsibility of the chief executive officer. In recognition of these relationships, some governments group personnel functions (including labor relations) together with other top staff functions, such as planning and budgeting, in a general department of administration that reports to the chief executive officer. **The chief executive officer of the government should establish clear divisions of authority and mechanisms for coordination in the making and execution of personnel policy among the offices responsible for planning, finance, budget, management analysis and control, legal affairs, and personnel support functions.**

Evaluating Personnel Support Functions

Just as support is growing for more precise evaluation of the effectiveness of government programs, so there is greater recognition that the support functions of government should also be regularly evaluated to determine and improve their effectiveness. **We recommend that governments establish clear goals and objectives for personnel management support functions and the various components (such as recruitment, selection, and classification) that relate to their effectiveness in meeting the broader purposes of government and identify indicators by which their effectiveness can be regularly evaluated.**

We recognize that in this regard, the rapid growth and numerous changes in the nature of public employment in recent years have created a substantially new situation for governments. Although we attempt in this statement to highlight some of the key relationships and important considerations, we realize that the ramifications of these changes are far from fully understood. The evolution of satisfactory personnel policies and practices will result principally from experimentation by state and local governments. However, much can be done in the meantime. **We encourage personnel specialists to work more closely with universities and other research organizations to identify more systematically areas of research that will add to what is currently a limited store of descriptive and analytic data on modern public personnel management.**

Chapter 4

COLLECTIVE BARGAINING *

TRADITIONALLY, THE TERMS OF PUBLIC EMPLOYMENT were set unilaterally by governments, and employees could either accept them or seek work elsewhere. In recent years, many state and local governments have adopted collective bargaining at the prompting of employee organizations. A rising proportion of public employees now participate in setting the terms of their employment through formal and legally structured negotiations with their government employers. Collective bargaining for state and local employees was given a major boost in 1962 with President Kennedy's Executive Order 10988, which supported union recognition and meet-and-confer status for federal employees on many nonwage matters.

Collective bargaining is not necessarily the best, the only, or the inevitable model for labor relations in the public sector. It has the undesirable consequence of casting labor-management relations in an adversary mold, thereby emphasizing the differences between those who presumably lead and those who presumably are led in providing public services. Employees who otherwise would think of themselves as work-

*See memoranda by WILLIAM F. MAY and ROBERT F. NATHAN, pages 126 and 127.

ing in concert with their superiors may be encouraged to recognize and nurture their different interests, and the sense of joint effort by the entire public service on behalf of the public may thereby be diminished.

Nevertheless, collective bargaining in government may hold potential advantages. It can provide a practical means of containing conflict and encouraging peaceful resolution, especially in those instances in which employees have legitimate grievances concerning inadequate pay, poor working conditions, or inept management. In large governments, collective bargaining can be a means of assuring that individual employee concerns are not overlooked as a consequence of bureaucratic indifference. It may also provide a flexibility in adjusting personnel systems to meet changing management needs, a flexibility that is difficult to achieve when personnel policy is fixed by legislation. Collective bargaining has been demonstrated to be workable in certain governments if it is properly structured and appropriately adapted to the special conditions of the public sector in general and the individual jurisdictions in particular.

Even for governments where it has been adopted, collective bargaining cannot be assumed to be the ultimate structure for labor relations. Employees in the public sector, like employees in the private sector, have on rare occasions opted for decertification of a union or employee association that acted as the bargaining agent. The future may also reveal that collective bargaining was a stage in the evolution of labor-management relations that ultimately led to a structure that better served the interests of the public and government employees.

Public officials in jurisdictions that do not have collective bargaining have the opportunity to provide leadership in creating a positive atmosphere for the public service that employees may find preferable to collective bargaining. However, those same jurisdictions should also be prepared to confront the question of whether and how to adopt collective bargaining if it becomes desirable or necessary to do so. We encourage those jurisdictions that already have collective bargaining to reexamine its structure to assure that it supports effective and efficient government.

Our proposals for structuring the collective bargaining process are not meant to imply a judgment on the relative merits of collective bargaining. Rather, they reflect our belief that practicality dictates that when confronted with adopting collective bargaining, governments must structure it in the best way possible to serve the legitimate interests of both the public and public employees.

LEGAL FRAMEWORK

In 1935, the National Labor Relations Act (NLRA) gave the right to organize and bargain collectively to most workers in the private sector but excluded employees in the public sector. In the absence of federal guidance, the responsibility for establishing the framework for state-local labor relations has fallen to the state governments. When there has been no clear state guidance, that responsibility has fallen to local jurisdictions. In some cities, meet-and-confer or collective bargaining relationships originally developed by direct action of city or county councils or by order of the elected executive, without state statutes. In jurisdictions that do not formally provide for collective bargaining, associations or unions representing employees often negotiate informally with management.

Proponents of federal legislation establishing collective bargaining for state and local governments argue that the states have lagged in their responsibility to assure equal treatment for public employees and that the diversity among states in public labor relations is confusing and disruptive. Proposals for federal involvement vary. One approach is to expand the NLRA to include public employees. A second is federal enactment of a national public labor relations law that would parallel the NLRA in many respects, including the creation of a national board for public employees similar to the National Labor Relations Board. Proponents of both approaches argue that public employees should have the same right to bargain collectively as their counterparts in the private sector, although those favoring the second approach believe that there are sufficient differences between public and private employees to necessitate separate laws and mechanisms for each. A third approach would have the federal government establish minimum standards requiring the states to adopt laws granting public employees the right to bargain. States that did not comply within a given period of time would be subject to judicial proceedings that might result in temporary federal administration of public-sector labor relations or loss of federal funding.

We believe that although an argument can be made for federal legislation, the authority should be left to the states to determine the legal framework for state and local government labor relations in their jurisdictions. The states are in a better position than the federal government to create and develop a structure that best accounts for the variable economic, organizational, and especially, political conditions that so importantly affect public-sector labor relations. The same set of powers that may remedy the unfair weakness of public employees in one jurisdiction may unduly strengthen public employees in another. State legislatures are more familiar with the conditions and needs of their own state governments and the local governments that they have created and therefore could make adjustments more easily if conditions changed or experience showed the need for modification. The states should experiment in this complex and rapidly changing area. Such experimentation would assure that different approaches would be tried and innovations would be facilitated, and in this way, states could learn from one another what seems to work best.

Our preference for state responsibility is also partly predicated on principles of federalism. The federal system traditionally encouraged state and local responsibility in matters of public policy in the belief not only that such decisions are best made by the people closest to the need and most directly affected by the action chosen but also that power should be decentralized wherever possible to guard against the potential abuses that result from overly centralized control. Clearly, an appropriate balance must be struck between the power of the states and the responsibility of the federal government to assure constitutional guarantees and promote the national interest. In this age of prominent government activity at all levels and rapid and complex social and economic change, it is difficult to define where that balance lies, which way it is inclined, and what actions will affect it in the future. Nevertheless, it is our belief that given the concentration of power in Washington that has occurred over the past several decades and indications that the national government has reached limits in its ability to deal with the diversity of conditions in various states and localities, the states should exercise responsibility in areas of public policy in which a compelling reason for federal action cannot be demonstrated. In our judgment, state and local government labor relations is one such area.

This does not suggest that we believe the federal government is constitutionally precluded from legislating in the area of state-local labor relations. Such recent Supreme Court decisions as the *National League of Cities* v. *Usery*[1] have had the effect of limiting congressional influence on matters of state and local government employment policy under the

---

1. 426 U.S. 833 (1976).

commerce clause, but they have stopped short of reversing historic decisions by the Court that recognize congressional authority to regulate state and local activity under other clauses of the Constitution, such as the spending clause, as well as under the commerce clause with respect to nontraditional government functions. The current Court has shown a preference, although a divided one, for state determination. Nevertheless, to what extent and in what measure Congress has the constitutional authority to regulate state and local government labor relations will remain an open question until it is confronted by the Supreme Court, probably on a case-by-case basis.

Although we favor leaving responsibility for public labor relations with the states, we also recognize that the absence of a legal framework in some states and the existence of unsatisfactory legislation in others perpetuates confusion and conflict and risks compounding the problems of labor-management relations in government. **We urge state governments to take legislative action that will provide a workable framework for labor relations in the interest of improving government performance, resolutely supporting the merit principle in public employment, and protecting the rights of employees.**

For those states that have adopted or that decide to adopt a legal framework for labor relations that includes collective bargaining, we recommend the guidelines set forth in the remainder of this chapter.

ADMINISTRATION OF LABOR RELATIONS

States that permit or require bargaining with public employees need a statewide mechanism to assure compliance by the state government and its subdivisions with the structure and process for labor relations established by law. Even if federal legislation is passed, the states could still be given the principal responsibility for administering the law in accordance with federal requirements and guidelines. Likewise, state laws could decentralize some administrative responsibilities to local jurisdictions. Larger cities and counties, in particular, may properly exercise responsibility for determining their own bargaining units, holding elections to determine representation, and adjudicating claims of unfair practices, with supervision by, and appeals to, a state board. **We recommend that states which provide for collective bargaining with public employees create impartial state public-employee relations boards** charged with the following responsibilities as defined by appropriate statutory guidelines:

- determining bargaining units

- establishing the rules governing recognition and certification of employee organizations to represent the bargaining unit

- conducting elections to determine representation

- adjudicating unfair labor practices

- facilitating the resolution of impasses

- establishing other rules and regulations necessary to protect employee rights and the public interest

These responsibilities should be discharged in a manner that is consistent with the board's role as a quasi-judicial administrative agency.

The effectiveness of such boards depends, of course, upon the quality of people appointed to them. Such positions are always susceptible to patronage appointment with little regard for qualifications. Unqualified or biased appointees would quickly undermine the credibility and effectiveness of the board and of public labor relations in general.

DETERMINATION OF BARGAINING UNITS AND REPRESENTATION

A bargaining unit is a group of employees represented by a single employee organization for the purpose of negotiating with management. The unit may include an entire agency, a division within an agency, or a group of employees that is defined by occupation and that constitutes only part of an agency or transcends agency lines.

In general, a multiplicity of bargaining units is not conducive to effective collective bargaining. Such a pattern not only consumes inordinate amounts of time, money, and energy in bargaining but also encourages bargaining by comparison, attempts to catch up, and leapfrogging by one unit of gains made by another. Jurisdictions with many units usually established them prior to granting collective bargaining rights, when employee organizations were confined to meet-and-confer relationships and hence fragmentation was not so debilitating. However, large bargaining units do have disadvantages: They may limit the ability of bargaining to take into account differences among employee groups and agency operations, and they may unduly concentrate the power of employee organizations.

In most large jurisdictions, bargaining units might appropriately be designed to coincide with each of the major occupational groups of employees, such as police officers, fire fighters, and teachers. In other cases, units may correspond to major departmental divisions. It may also be appropriate in certain instances to establish variations of traditional bargaining units. For example, New York City provides for multiunit bargaining, in which certain topics common to large groups of employees are bargained at higher levels than topics of particular interest to smaller groups of employees. Multijurisdictional bargaining, in which a number of governments join together to bargain collectively with their employees, is another alternative; some jurisdictions in Minnesota have instituted multijurisdictional bargaining, although the results of this experiment are still inconclusive. In Britain, public employees in local government bargain certain items on a nationwide basis.

Hawaii and Wisconsin have laws stipulating the structure of bargaining units; however, most states with collective bargaining have developed criteria to be followed by administrative agencies in establishing units. In some cases, bargaining units have developed on an ad hoc, case-by-case basis as bargaining has been extended to additional employees. **Although we believe that the appropriate structure of bargaining units depends principally upon local circumstances, such structures should, in general, be broadly drawn to encompass a clear and identifiable community of interest among the employees included and should be designed to minimize fragmentation and to avoid impeding operating efficiency or inhibiting reorganization in accordance with changing management goals.**

The structure of bargaining units can also have an impact on the effectiveness of middle management and supervisory personnel. In order to assure strong management direction and to have the ability to administer negotiated contracts, bona fide supervisory personnel should be considered part of management, dealt with as management, and encouraged to think of themselves as management. In the event of a strike or other job action, it is especially important that supervisory personnel

be clearly allied with management so that they can be counted on to help provide a minimum level of essential services. **We believe that supervisory personnel should be considered part of management and consequently should not be included in bargaining units.** In those instances in which supervisory personnel do have bargaining rights, they should not be included in the same bargaining unit or belong to the same organization as nonsupervisory personnel.

In general, we would define a supervisor as someone who is responsible for directing the work of subordinates; who has an effective voice in determining whether subordinates are promoted, disciplined, or discharged; or who acts in a capacity representing management interests. Because situations vary according to the size and function of the public services being provided, the determination of whether an individual is a bona fide supervisor and thus excluded from a bargaining unit should be made on a case-by-case basis. For example, most school vice-principals should be considered management and hence should not bargain. However, in larger school districts, vice-principals may find themselves far down the administrative ladder and may feel less like management than like relatively powerless employees in need of a collective voice to protect their interests in relation to higher levels of management. The same is often the case with supervisory police and fire officers. The key consideration is that management must retain a clear identity and certainty of control over the top echelons of public personnel.

In keeping with the practice of collective bargaining in the private sector, we believe that exclusive recognition should be given to one employee association or union to bargain for all members of the bargaining unit. However, precautions should be taken both to guarantee that no employee will be forced to join a union against his or her wishes and to assure that union representation is genuinely democratic and responsive to the changing desires of employees. **We recommend that the bargaining agent be selected by secret ballot of all employees in the bargaining unit in elections held by the state public-employee relations board upon petition of a substantial proportion of public employees. However, no employee should be required to join the association or union elected as the bargaining agent.** Whether employees not belonging to the union should be required to pay a fee in lieu of dues (i.e., whether there should be an agency shop) should be determined by the states. The states, in turn, might decide the issue through legislation or might permit the matter to be decided through local legislation or negotiation.

DEFINING MANAGEMENT

Determining who bargains for the public employer is complicated by the division of authority among the three branches of government and within the executive branch itself.

Division of Authority among the Branches of Government

Successful bargaining requires that management's bargaining agent (almost always a representative of the executive branch) be reasonably assured that agreements made at the bargaining table will be honored. Negotiated agreements that fail to win top executive or legislative support undermine both management's credibility and the bargaining process; labor is forced into end-running to whatever official or legislative body possesses the power to give them what they think they deserve or have won at the bargaining table. Nevertheless, state legislatures and local government councils have, and should retain, both the authority and the responsibility to assure that decisions and actions of the executive branch conform to the public interest as defined by the legislative body.

Relationship between the Executive and Legislative Branches

The chief executive may theoretically represent the public at the bargaining table, but as a practical matter, there is a limit to the ability of one elected official to understand, absorb, and synthesize the wide diversity of political interests in a state, county, or city. There are numerous third parties whose stakes in bargaining may be greater than the interest of the public at large, for example, the parents of students, citizens highly dependent on police services, or elderly people dependent on social services. Yet, the interests of such groups are not represented directly at the bargaining table; rather, they are represented indirectly through the management negotiator, whose commitment to specific third-party interests may be diffused by his or her concern for the nebulously defined public interest or for other matters. Because they lack more direct involvement in the bargaining process, such third parties tend to look to legislative bodies to protect their interests. As a representative body, legislators and city and county council members also reflect the interest of public employees (who are voters) in proportion to the employees' political influence in their jurisdiction.

The conflict poses a serious challenge to collective bargaining in government: Viable bargaining requires that the representative of management have the power to make enforceable agreements, but the legislative body has a role as guardian of the broader, more diverse public interest.

We believe that as a general principle, the executive branch should be responsible for representing government in labor relations and should be granted wide latitude by the legislative body to negotiate and implement agreements. However, the legitimate interest and responsibility of the legislative body to assure that agreements are in accord with their interpretation of the public interest, including the fiscal limitations on government, should also be acknowledged and provided for. Ideally, agreements made by the executive in accordance with general guidelines approved by the legislative body should be subject to limited oversight by the legislative branch. One step that the legislative body might take is the identification of a focal point for liaison with the executive branch in matters pertaining to labor relations. That focal point might be a joint committee of both houses with substantial latitude to work with the executive branch to develop and implement personnel policy. In the end, however, there are no simple mechanisms to resolve the conflict and balance the responsibilities of the two branches. A tradition of workable and reasonable interaction must be established between the two branches in matters of labor relations.

Role of the Judiciary

The judicial branch has been increasingly drawn into public labor relations not just to settle disputes but also occasionally to define the mission and operating procedures of public agencies as a precondition for resolving labor problems. We view this development with alarm because it signals one more instance in which decisions that should properly be made by political or administrative institutions are being made by the courts. The problem results from several factors, including ambiguous statutes that require judicial interpretation or overly specific laws that are inapplicable to situations that arise subsequently, the reluctance of political and administrative officials to make unpopular decisions, the overwillingness of some judges to decide issues that are political matters or that they are technically unprepared to comprehend fully, and the eagerness of litigants and lawyers to pursue every legal remedy. The continued erosion of executive authority and responsibility by constant recourse to the courts could undermine the effectiveness not just of public labor relations but of government performance in general. **We strongly urge that state and local governments counteract the danger of overreliance on the courts in public labor relations by more careful crafting of public labor law; by greater reliance on institutions, such as public-employee relations boards, that have the expertise and authority to resolve labor disputes; and by encouraging the courts themselves to be highly selective in determining which pleadings they will consider.**

Responsibility within the Executive Branch

Responsibility within the executive branch is often divided among the nominal chief executive (the elected governor, mayor, or county executive or the top appointed professional manager) and other officers who may be independently elected or have separate statutory authority for legal, financial, civil service, or personnel matters, each of which is relevant to collective bargaining. **We believe that the chief executive officer, whether an elected governor, mayor, or county executive or an appointed professional manager, should represent the government in collective bargaining through a professional negotiator and should assume responsibility for coordinating those other elements of the executive branch that bear some relation to the bargaining process and its outcome.** Experience has shown that the chief executive officer generally should not become an active member of the bargaining team; rather, he or she should be represented by someone experienced in public-sector labor relations. It is also important that negotiators be in close contact with operating department heads both in preparing for negotiations and during negotiations so that management's position and the resulting contract fully take into account possible impact on work rules, pay, safety provisions, and other factors affecting management of public services.

The responsibility of the chief executive in larger jurisdictions can best be exercised through a labor relations office that would negotiate and administer agreements and represent management before mediators, fact finders, arbitrators, and other bodies such as state boards and the courts. **To carry out its tasks, the labor relations office should be staffed with or otherwise use professional negotiators and researchers who have a knowledge of the range of issues relevant to public-sector labor relations, including civil service and personnel regulations and administrative practices, financial and budget operations, the manage-**

LIMITS TO JUDICIAL RESOLUTION

The Pennsylvania Public Employees Relations Act (195) of 1970 provides that strikes by most public employees (with the exception of policemen, fire fighters, prison guards, and court employees) "shall not be prohibited unless or until such a strike creates a clear and present danger or threat to the health, safety or welfare of the public." (Article X, Section 1003.) The judge confronted with interpreting this language as it applied to striking teachers in Philadelphia in 1972 complained that:

"The court is called upon to digest the economic, professional and managerial complexities of an educational system, assume problems unresolved by mediation and/or fact-finding commissions, and decide what is in the best interests of the public or presents a clear and present danger thereto." (Such language) "takes the judiciary beyond its obligation of interpreting the law to the field of legislating."

Source: Bernard C. Brominski, "From the Perspective of the Local Judge," quoted in Hugh D. Jascourt, "Limited Right to Strike Laws—Can They Work When Applied to Public Education?" in Trends in Public Sector Labor Relations, eds. Arvid Anderson and Hugh D. Jascourt, vol. 1 (Washington, D.C.: International Personnel Management Association, 1972–1973), pp. 150, 153.

ment needs of line agencies, and legal matters. Public employers have increasingly recognized the need for professional expertise in labor relations, and their associations have established specialized service agencies, such as the Labor-Management Relations Service of the U.S. Conference of Mayors, to provide guidance to member governments in developing professional capability in labor relations. In 1972, the National Public Employer Labor Relations Association (NPELRA) was formed as a professional organization for the growing number of full-time labor relations personnel in government.

The development of professional capability in contract administration, not only in staff agencies specializing in employee relations but also in management and first-line supervision, is equally important. Success in employee relations is not just a matter of periodic formal bargaining; it requires day-to-day effort and sensitivity to the detail of negotiated contracts and needs of employees. Such attention can be given only on the job by managers and supervisors.

Semi-Independent School Boards

A special problem arises in those instances in which separately elected boards of education are responsible for setting school policy and bargaining with teachers and other school employees but are dependent on the city or county council or state government for funding. It is unrealistic in this age of tight finances and policy interdependence to expect the funding body to accept and act on agreements made by the school board without questioning both the cost and the effectiveness of the educational program. Yet, such dual responsibility creates obvious difficulties at the bargaining table. A school board may agree to a wage increase for teachers that the city or county council refuses to fund. The board then has no recourse but to cut programs in order to finance negotiated wage increases or else to renege on the contract. The teachers, having no direct bargaining relationship with the city or county council, are forced to accept the reneging or to apply political pressure directly to the city or county council.

One way to resolve the problem is to combine policy-making and taxing authority, either by giving school boards their own taxing authority or by fully incorporating school districts into the general-purpose government. However, each approach would forfeit the current advantage of maintaining a semi-independent school board with responsibility for education policy but linked to broader policy concerns by its dependence on the city or county council for financing. A partial solution might be to involve the funding jurisdiction more directly in negotiations between the school board and its employees on a consultative basis in order to enhance the likelihood that agreements will be honored by the funding jurisdiction. More generally, tax-raising authorities need to develop the capacity to analyze school board budgets and programs more effectively in order to ensure that the public moneys they appropriate for education are being spent effectively, efficiently, and in harmony with other public programs. Alternatively, school boards might be given a revenue limit within which they would allocate their budget priorities, and they would be expected to justify any inability to stay within that revenue limit.

BARGAINING PROCESS

Some of the principles that govern the bargaining process in the private sector (e.g., requirements for explicit procedures, good-faith bargaining, and the definition and adjudication of unfair labor practices) are generally applicable to the public sector. However, important adaptations are required. As we noted earlier, not only labor and management but also numerous third-party groups have a stake in the negotiations. Taxpayers are concerned about costs, and service recipients are concerned about implications for the level and quality of public services. **We believe that the process of collective bargaining in government should be structured to assure the public's right to be informed about the issues under negotiation and the full costs and fiscal implications of settlements, both short term and long term, before final agreements are approved and adopted by management.** There are several ways that this might be accomplished, depending on local circumstances.

Bargaining sessions might be opened to the public. Experience has demonstrated that although it has drawbacks, such sunshine bargaining is workable and can be beneficial. Professional negotiators representing both labor and management contend that sessions open to the public would result in grandstanding on both sides, which would be incompatible with serious and effective bargaining. Proponents argue that the greater visibility would decrease the likelihood of government giveaways and would make the public more familiar with the details of issues being negotiated.

An alternative to completely open bargaining sessions is the creation of formal procedures for providing the public with fuller information on the substance of negotiations. For example, initial bargaining sessions, including the presentation of opening positions of both labor and management, might be open to the public and might permit comment by interested third parties. Subsequent bargaining would then be closed to the public, but the final tentative agreement would be made public before being signed. As a practical matter, any requirement for a structure designed to assure totally open bargaining is likely to force labor and management negotiators into surreptitious bargaining to reach agreements. Therefore, the key principle is that the public be fully informed about the formal positions of both sides and the potential outcomes of bargaining before final agreements are executed.

The bargaining process should also be integrated with the government's budget process to assure that negotiators are fully informed about budgetary projections as a guide to negotiation and that contracts requiring additional funding can be adequately accounted for in the budget for the coming fiscal year.

SCOPE OF BARGAINING

The impact of collective bargaining on the cost of government and on public policy and operations is one of the more volatile and critical issues in public-sector labor relations. Wages, benefits, hours, and conditions of work, the items traditionally subject to bargaining in the private sector, are generally legitimate items of bargaining in the state-local sector as well, although some labor relations experts argue that states and localities should follow the lead of the federal government in not bargaining over wages and benefits.

Conditions of Work

Working conditions typically include safety factors, shift schedules, vacations and breaks, comfort, and work load, all matters of appropriate concern to employees. They generally do not include topics related to policy or management concerns, such as agency goals and objectives, strategies and procedures for accomplishing work, and organization of offices. However, conditions of work are often difficult to distinguish from matters of agency policy or operation. For example, teacher organizations argue that class size is a bargainable item because the greater the number of students, the greater the stress on a teacher; school boards retort that class size is a question of policy and resource allocation and thus the preserve of management. **In enacting or revising public-sector collective bargaining legislation, states should identify the**

CALCULATING
THE COST OF LABOR AGREEMENTS

The Resource Allocation Model (RAM) used for budget forecasting purposes is used to perform a number of analyses during labor negotiations. By using RAM with the personnel/payroll data base, we can analyze any mix of requests, and by using historical costs, project the impact of proposed changes. We know the number and types of positions covered by each bargaining group and exactly what we have been paying for. Since we also know the number of authorized but vacant positions, we can determine the impact of any staff reductions which might be required to compensate for cost increases.

We also calculate the cost of proposed changes by fund source. This calculation tells us whether the individual fund can absorb the costs, if any would have to be underwritten by other sources or, in the case of our utilities, if the changes would trigger a rate increase.

The variety of analyses we can and do make with RAM is almost endless. It has become an invaluable tool and has enabled us to more realistically deal with the various unions representing our work forces.

Our 1977 collective bargaining negotiations have highlighted the need for rapid and accurate long-range calculations. Studies are now underway to determine the feasibility of having a terminal available at the bargaining sessions for instantaneous computations.

Source: "How Dayton Uses Computers to Live Within Her Budget and Enhance Delivery of Services," *Public Management* (December 1977).

topics subject to bargaining and should also stipulate those management prerogatives not subject to bargaining. Moreover, management should be consistently vigilant in retaining and preserving its prerogatives in negotiations.

Management Prerogatives

In general, management prerogatives include those powers necessary to manage the work force in carrying out government policy effectively and efficiently. Although the specific prerogatives may vary, they generally include such items as

● agency goals and objectives

● approaches to meeting goals and objectives, including contracting

● the work to be performed, how it is to be performed, and the standards or measures by which it is to be evaluated

● organizational structure

● the tools, machines, and equipment necessary to perform the work

● budgets and appropriations for agencies and programs

● selection of supervisors

● the need for increasing or decreasing the complement of employees or for overtime work

● employment standards, selection of new employees, assignment and promotion policies, and discipline, all of which should be stipulated by law to be based exclusively on standards of merit

Disagreement invariably arises over the distinction between management prerogatives and conditions of work. In some instances, the two are inseparable; in other cases, changes undertaken by management may have an impact on working conditions. To the greatest extent possible, such disagreements should be resolved through normal bargaining and impasse procedures.

Some employee groups argue that agency policies, goals, and objectives are the appropriate concern of employees, whether or not they directly affect conditions of work. Thus, teachers contend that as professional educators, they have the knowledge, the responsibility, and the right to have some voice in determining the curriculum and the process by which they teach their students and that such matters are appropriate issues for negotiation. Similarly, social workers in New York went on strike in 1965 partly over the allegedly low levels of welfare services to their clients. **Although there are circumstances in which it would be** beneficial to both management and labor for employees to participate in some aspects of agency planning and policy making, we do not believe that the collective bargaining process is the appropriate mechanism for such participation. Formal collective bargaining should be confined as much as possible to resolving issues over which labor and management tend to have natural adversary positions, such as wages, benefits, hours, and conditions of work. **Cooperation toward development of mutually beneficial goals and operating procedures, including such formal mechanisms as labor-management committees, should be encouraged but should remain outside the formal collective bargaining process in a nonadversary environment.** (We return to this question in Chapter 6.)

Productivity

Distinguishing between areas of adversary and cooperative relations is, of course, a less than precise matter. The two overlap and in some instances are inseparable, as in bargaining over issues that affect agency productivity. Most productivity improvements result more from changes initiated and financed by management (e.g., improvements in

---

BARGAINING OPEN TO THE PUBLIC:
Mixed Reaction in Florida

There is no question that bargaining in a "goldfish bowl" inhibits compromise, lengthens the bargaining process timewise, is more expensive, creates controversy and fosters additional unnecessary adversary relations. The results of this study indicate, however, that even with all of these disadvantages, School Board members, superintendents, the public news media, and, at least superficially, some teacher unions believe that "goldfish bowl" collective bargaining should be retained.

Source: Donald R. Magruder, *Bargaining in Public: Help or Hindrance?* (Washington, D.C.: Labor-Management Relations Service, U.S. Conference of Mayors, 1976), p. 11.

capital, equipment, organization, or work procedures) than from greater effort by workers. Differences in employee skill levels, responsibility, and performance should be reflected in salary differentials (see Chapter 6). **Bargaining with respect to agency productivity should be strictly confined to exchanging specific, one-time financial payments for actual or anticipated increases in productivity that reflect employees' actual contributions to those increases.**

There are two ways in which money might legitimately be exchanged for specific employee actions leading to productivity improvements:

First, financial incentive systems, commonly called *gain sharing*, might be used. Under such systems, specific increases in productivity are quantitatively measured and clearly related to extra effort on the part of employees. The financial reward should be in the form of lump-sum cash payments or bonuses related to documented quantitative improvement in productivity, not in permanent wage or benefit increases that would result in perpetuated payments in excess of, and extending beyond, employee contributions to increased productivity.

Second, management might, in certain circumstances, agree to financial payment in exchange for labor's agreement to changes in operations that management believes will lead to increased productivity. This approach calls for caution and discretion. It does not suggest that labor should be compensated for every change in work procedures. Such changes are, and should remain, the prerogative and the responsibility of management. However, it does recognize that some changes can be facilitated if labor exerts unusual effort or sustains unusual hardship during the transition and that it may be in the interest of management and a legitimate demand of labor to recognize or encourage that extra effort with a cash payment. But here again, the exchange should be a one-time payment precisely related to labor's contribution. Once the changeover is accomplished, any additional compensation due to labor in general or to individual employees should be determined by the same criteria used to establish wage levels in general.

In the private sector, wage levels in any given industry have risen more in relation to productivity increases in the economy as a whole than in relation to productivity increases in that particular industry. Comparable jobs in industries with radically different achievements in productivity still tend to pay comparable salaries. There are, to be sure, differentials that reflect the ability of more productive industries to pay higher wages for similar jobs; but presumably, the higher wages attract more capable or motivated employees.

CAUTIONS IN PRODUCTIVITY BARGAINING

The CSEA (Civil Service Employees Association) argued that the new commitment to productivity bargaining prohibited unilateral action by the State to reschedule shifts of individuals, establish new shifts, or change the starting and closing times.

Individual workers picked up the theme and soon union officials were "under increasing pressure from employees to resist changes in individual assignments and to utilize the productivity clause as the vehicle to prevent the implementation of myriad changes in terms and conditions of employment." Agency heads soon found that "virtually every change in State work procedures seemed to be viewed (by employees) as an application of 'productivity bargaining' and to be resisted on that ground alone."

Source: Melvin H. Osterman, Jr., "Productivity Bargaining in New York State—What Went Wrong?" (An occasional paper of the Institute of Public Employment, New York State School of Industrial and Labor Relations, Cornell University, Ithaca, N.Y., 1975), p. 20.

Similarly, in the public sector, there is no reason why an accountant in a city water department that rapidly increases its productivity should, as a consequence of that increase, be given a higher salary than a comparably classified and skilled accountant in the finance department, where productivity remains unchanged. However, the accountant in the water department might well be given a cash payment in exchange for, and limited to, superlative effort on his or her part.

IMPASSE RESOLUTION

If collective bargaining is to work, provision must be made for the resolution of impasses that recognizes the rights, legitimate interests, and power both of labor and of management as the representative of the public. The most desirable way to resolve impasses is for both sides to reopen negotiations and bargain until they reach an agreement or to employ neutral third parties to help break the deadlock. If such efforts do not succeed, more formal steps are required. **The responsibility for resolving, or facilitating the resolution of, impasses in collective bargaining should be given to a neutral agency that is professionally staffed, adequately compensated, and equipped with a range of mechanisms for settling, or facilitating the settlement of, public-sector labor disputes.** Such responsibility might be given to the public-employee relations board or lodged in a separate agency committed exclusively to dispute resolution. Creation of a separate agency may enhance the perception of neutrality, although public-employee relations boards might accomplish the same purpose by establishing a separate division for providing mediators, fact finders, and arbitrators or lists of professionals experienced in public-sector dispute resolution.

The dispute-resolution mechanisms for which the agency should be equipped include the following:

- *Mediation.* A mediator is a neutral third party who attempts to conciliate disputes between labor and management but does not have the power to enforce a settlement.

- *Fact-finding.* A fact finder (or panel of fact finders) is a neutral third party who hears the cases presented by each side, often in a formal proceeding, and generally makes specific recommendations for resolving the dispute. Fact-finding is typically the second step after mediation has failed.

- *Arbitration.* An arbitrator is a neutral third party who goes beyond fact-finding to decide in favor of one side or the other. In binding arbitration, the decision of the arbitrator is final. *(Interest arbitration* refers to resolution of impasses arising in bargaining; *grievance arbitration* refers to the settlement of disputes in interpretation of a contract that has already been executed.) In last-offer arbitration, the arbitrator must find in favor of the last offer (or separable items in the last offer) presented by each of the parties; this presumably encourages each side to bargain seriously and to be reasonable in their positions in the knowledge that an unreasonable offer will result in the adoption of the other side's proposal.

Seventeen states now provide for arbitration of collective bargaining impasses. However, compulsory and binding arbitration is typically opposed by managers who fear that these mechanisms provide a third party who is unfamiliar with local conditions and unaccountable to local authority with the power to bind government to costly settlements. In 1978, Dayton, Ohio, voters rejected a proposal to submit future impasses in bargaining with fire fighters to arbitration even though the city had recently suffered a strike by fire fighters.

Two other mechanisms for resolving impasses are designed to involve the public or its elected representatives more directly in the resolution of labor-management impasses.

● *Public Referendum.* Public referendum to settle impasses by placing the issue on a ballot for a formal vote by the electorate is one approach to increasing public participation or assuring that agreements are in accord with the public interest as defined by the electorate. Its disadvantages include the technical problems of putting complicated contract issues on a ballot, the delays in settlement pending elections, and the danger of further politicizing labor disputes.

● *Legislative Approval.* Some propose an increased role for legislative bodies, specifically that city and county councils and state legislatures review and approve or reserve the right to veto all contracts or contract provisions. Legislative bodies or their representatives might also assume responsibility for final action in resolving disputes.

Preoccupation with the techniques of resolving bargaining impasses or other labor disputes should not divert attention from a more fundamental source of labor peace, that is, mutual respect between employees and management based on good day-to-day working relationships and concern for the legitimate interests of both sides. (In Chapters 5 and 6, we suggest points to consider in establishing such a relationship.) Nevertheless, building a tradition of harmonious employee relations depends upon the existence of fair and workable arrangements for resolving disputes.

Similarly, preoccupation with the issue of public-employee strikes should not divert attention from the task of establishing workable mechanisms for dispute resolution. However, achieving peaceful dispute resolution depends in part upon how the issue of strikes is handled.

PUBLIC-EMPLOYEE STRIKES*

Eight states (Alaska, Hawaii, Minnesota, Montana, Oregon, Pennsylvania, Vermont, and Wisconsin) have granted certain classes of public employees a limited right to strike through specifically adopted legislation or judicial decisions (see Appendix D). In contrast, legal prohibition of public-employee strikes has not necessarily prevented them from occurring. There were 254 strikes or work stoppages by public employees in 1968, a seventeenfold increase over the number in 1958; yet, during that period, no state gave an unqualified right to strike.[2] In the year ending October 1975, there were 490 work stoppages or strikes, even though strikes continued to be prohibited in forty-five states. (See Figure 6.)

Any strike, whether legal or illegal, that disrupts a public service creates inconvenience, breeds mistrust and bad feelings, and may threaten immediate and irreparable injury to life and property. However, given the reality that some states permit strikes and that legal prohibition of strikes, apparently no matter how severe the penalties, cannot be enforced with complete certainty in the face of public employees determined to walk off their jobs, we suggest that the issue be approached in a practical manner. **We urge governments to take action to assure that strikes by public employees, whether legal or illegal, do not prevent government from meeting its fundamental responsibilities to protect public health, safety, and welfare.**

There are two ways to keep public-employee strikes from damaging the public interest: to prevent strikes from occurring and to limit their power to cause damage when they do occur.

Historically, governments have relied almost exclusively on deterrence; they have legally prohibited public employees from striking and have threatened sanctions for breaking the law. For a long time, this

---

2. Advisory Commission on Intergovernmental Relations, *Labor-Management Policies for State and Local Government* (Washington, D.C., 1969), p. 27.

*See memorandum by W. D. DANCE, page 128.

Figure 6: State and Local Government Work Stoppages, by Function, October 1975 to October 1976

Function	Number of Work Stoppages	Employees Involved		Duration (days)		Days of Idleness (employees × days)	
		Total	Average per Stoppage	Total	Average per Stoppage	Total	Average per Stoppage
Total	377	167,136	443	3,320	8.8	1,653,791	4,386.7
Education	184	84,466	459	1,740	9.5	915,725	4,976.8
Teachers	146	58,230	399	1,355	9.3	595,210	4,076.8
Other	98	26,236	268	1,067	10.9	320,515	3,270.6
Highways	65	6,619	102	590	9.1	62,021	954.2
Public welfare	17	7,796	459	195	11.5	87,843	5,167.2
Hospitals	17	25,513	1,501	242	14.2	123,039	7,237.6
Police protection	27	3,004	111	132	4.9	7,430	275.2
Fire protection	21	1,181	56	51	2.4	2,641	125.8
Sanitation	40	3,107	78	239	6.0	18,285	457.1
All other functions	118	35,450	300	1,010	8.6	436,807	3,701.8

Source: U.S. Bureau of the Census, *Labor-Management Relations in State and Local Governments: 1976*, State and Local Government Special Studies no. 88 (Washington, D.C.: U.S. Government Printing Office, 1978), p. 5.

policy was reasonably effective; but recently, the incidence of strikes began to rise. From 1958 to 1976, the number of working days lost because of public-employee strikes rose from 7,500 to 1.7 million, a rate of increase dramatically greater than the increase in the number of public employees. Strict penalties, which in the past were frequently overlooked when employees returned to work, are now applied with greater frequency. Although the more severe sanctions have had some effect, they have not prevented illegal strikes from occurring. Many governments that have relied solely on deterring strikes to prevent harm to the public have found themselves helpless to maintain a minimal level of essential public services when that policy failed.

In some instances, strict antistrike laws and their enforcement have proved counterproductive. More than once, jailed labor leaders have become instant martyrs and thereby strengthened the resolve of striking employees. Unsuccessful attempts by public officials to have the courts enjoin public employees against striking illegally have had the practical effect of legitimizing a strike in the eyes of employees and even in the eyes of the public. The courts in Michigan, New Hampshire, and Rhode Island have held that injunctions against strikes, even those prohibited by law, must rest on a demonstration of actual or likely irreparable injury. If injunctions are won but ignored, public officials face an unpleasant choice: prosecuting hundreds or thousands of public servants or winking at the law and thereby undermining the government's credibility. The most important weakness of sole reliance on deterrence through legal prohibition is that if employees still refuse to work after all remedies have been exhausted, the government's ability to meet its responsibilities to the public is impaired or totally crippled.

The blanket prohibition of strikes tends to overlook several factors that favor management in public-sector labor disputes:

First, work stoppages usually do not create financial pressure to settle as they do in business; on the contrary, tax revenues continue to flow in while wage payments cease (although additional costs may be incurred to pay for temporary assistance).

Second, the public reaction to a strike is felt by unions as well as by management. Many government officials feel that the public, tired of the perceived aggressiveness of some unions and the increased taxes that result from inflated wage settlements, will support them in their resolve not to give in to striking employees.

Third, in some cases, the inconvenience caused by work stoppages may be so minor that it calls the need for the striking employees into question. During a strike by Berkeley, California, fire fighters in 1975, the city manager observed that the skeleton contingency crew seemed capable of handling emergency calls and thereupon cut the size of the fire force. According to the city manager of Palo Alto, California, a 1975 strike by employees prompted supervisors to get "closer to the work and make changes in operations after the strike was over." He continued, "we discovered that we could do without some things on a permanent basis."[3] Some managers believe that in such instances, and even in those cases in which walkouts do create considerable inconvenience, it may be preferable to take a strike than to meet labor's demands or submit to arbitration that could result in excessively high wage costs.

Fourth, public employees are also dependent on government services, and they are themselves inconvenienced by strikes. For example, transit strikes keep sanitation workers from their jobs. In turn, when sanitation workers permit garbage to pile up in the streets, transit workers have to suffer the inconvenience along with everyone else.

The alternative to deterring strikes through legal prohibition is to limit the power of strikes, legal or illegal, to prevent government from meeting its obligations. Few municipal employees or union leaders consciously aim to inflict injury through strikes. Rather, they usually seek to cause sufficient public inconvenience so that their services will be missed, to create by their absence a heavy work load for those who substitute during walkouts so that the substitutes will pressure management to settle, or to demonstrate that a prolonged walkout may result in more severe consequences. **Management should make contingency plans to assure that government retains its capability to perform essential services in the event of a strike.** Supervisory and administrative personnel can assume essential line operation positions; workers can be temporarily shifted from other agencies; employees can be enlisted from other jurisdictions; in public safety strikes, other emergency personnel can be used; private contractors can be hired; citizens can lend their efforts. Such measures have been used effectively in dealing with strikes in virtually all municipal services, including police and fire protection.

---

3. *Public Management* (August 1976).

These two approaches, deterrence and limiting the power of public strikes to cause injury, can be mutually supportive. Legal prohibitions may be ineffective if government has no practical means for limiting damage when employees strike in violation of the law. Prior planning and preparation by the government to continue functioning in the face of a strike while also continuing to seek a negotiated settlement may in some instances prove to be a stronger deterrent to strikes than the threat of legal sanctions that inflict little pain or are not likely to be applied. If by having the ability to provide a minimal level of services in the event of a strike, management can limit the power of employees to disrupt public services or cause irreparable injury, the law may be used more sparingly and hence more effectively to deter truly harmful actions that no preventive measures can preclude. Public employees, like all citizens, are more likely to obey reasonable laws; moreover, the public is more likely to support government officials against employees who break reasonable laws. Laws that permit private fuel distributors to strike in winter but

TEACHER STRIKES AND MORAL RIGHTS

I've marched on picket lines. I believe in union power and collective bargaining. So did the Rev. Martin Luther King, Jr. That's why he was in Memphis, and I with him, on that day when the assassin's bullet struck him. We were there in support of a strike by Memphis's sanitation workers.

But as with all forms of power, union power has its traps and defeats. And no union's power must be handled more carefully and judiciously than that held by organized public employees.

The questions I'm raising about teachers' unions have nothing to do with collective bargaining or the right to strike. I support both, although they are outlawed in many places.

What I question is more important. A whole series of moral questions must be answered if organized teachers are to preserve their moral authority, their community mandate. Before they strike, they must consider:

•How clear is their right to strike if a preoccupation with guaranteed that deny library workers the right to strike are perceived as unreasonable. Laws that require striking employees, public or private, to return to their jobs in the face of real and imminent danger to the public are perceived as reasonable.

The power of public employees to cause irritation or inconvenience to the public need not be totally curbed. To do so would be excessively costly, even if it were possible. Such action might also unnecessarily deprive employees of a measure of power that it may be desirable for them to have in order to protect their own interests and dissuade them from seeking power through other routes. The more practical objectives are to limit the actual damage to public health, safety, or welfare that can be caused by strikes and to permit public employees a measure of power commensurate with their legitimate interests.

To accomplish this objective requires a range of measures tailored to the particular circumstances of different jurisdictions and different types of government services. The relative power of public employees to

employment usurps the objective of guaranteeing education?

•How clear is the right to strike when a union seeks contract protection for incompetence, and so undercuts the competent?

•How clear is the right to strike for more money when the employer—a taxpaying parent—holds tax receipts in one hand and test results in the other that prove he's paying more and more for less and less?

•And how clear is the right to strike when the union doesn't calculate what it will cost a child whose teacher walked out of the classroom?

. . . the question is less and less that of the legal right to strike and increasingly one of moral rights. And clearly it is moral rights that are the foundation of successful strikes and causes.

The prudent use of power is its best protection.

Source: Jesse L. Jackson, "Teacher Strikes and Moral Rights," *Washington Post,* May 19, 1977.

engage in effective job actions is determined by numerous factors, including the nature of the service they perform; their numbers, organization, and determination; the ability of employee organizations to exercise influence at all three levels of government; the relative political will of the public; the relative skill and capability of government managers; and the formal structure of labor relations. Adjustments are required according to particular circumstances so that a balance is achieved between the legitimate power of employees and the public interest. For some services in some jurisdictions, permitting public employees to strike within prescribed limits may pose little threat to the public; for other services, especially those involving public safety, there may be no alternative but to ban employee strikes and impose swift and effective sanctions in the event that the law is broken.

In the end, each state and its local jurisdictions must devise a policy and provide mechanisms for dispute resolution that are both practical and compatible with local circumstances. The goal should be to provide employees with sufficient power to negotiate on behalf of their legitimate interests without being able to threaten the public health, safety, or welfare. Such a negotiating structure appropriately balances the power of employees with the public interest and encourages greater reliance on bargaining and mediation to resolve impasses. It is also essential to building the tradition of trust and mutual respect that ultimately is the key to harmonious and productive labor relations.

Chapter 5

THE ROLE
OF THE MANAGER

PROVIDING A COHERENT AND EFFECTIVE STRUCTURE for personnel management is important, but it can do no more than establish the context within which top officials and managers assume responsibility for managing. In *Improving Productivity in State and Local Government*, we discussed the components of management that are required for better performance in government. In this statement, we are concerned with managers as public employees who are also responsible for managing the public work force.

The classical formula for getting good management in any organization is applicable to state and local government: Managers should first be given clear direction concerning the goals or objectives that they are responsible for achieving. This is especially important in government, where the translation of intangible goals into tangible and measurable objectives against which accomplishment can be assessed is particularly difficult. It is the responsibility of elected officials, working with professional managers, to translate vague political goals into specific managerial objectives. Assuming the existence of clear direction and an appropriate organizational framework, effective management requires finding people with the requisite managerial skills and abilities, giving them the resources and authority to do the job, and providing them with incentives that are related to performance.

QUALITY OF MANAGERS

During this century, the city management profession has developed a strong corps of capable managers with demonstrated ability. More than half of the nation's cities now employ professional chief executive officers. But even in those jurisdictions, managers other than the city manager frequently have little managerial training or experience. Many are functional professionals (e.g., police officers serving as police chiefs, doctors serving as directors of health departments, engineers heading public works agencies) who possess relevant and important specialized knowledge but who may have little experience or ability in managing large and complex organizations. Such people may be effective managers by nature or through experience, but often they are not.

Although some of the professions have begun to stress the importance of management and to include management training in the curriculum and development program of their professional schools and associations, there is some question about how effective that training is or how seriously it is taken.

The core of the problem is that managers tend to be appointed on the basis of political criteria, seniority, or civil service examinations that have little to do with management. **We recommend that top officials and legislative bodies establish procedures for effectively identifying, recruiting, and promoting people with managerial ability, based on criteria and assessment techniques that are predictive of managerial performance.** Strides have been made in recent years in developing the techniques of gauging such capability, including the use of assessment centers that test for a range of skills under simulated working conditions. It is equally important that top officials have sufficient flexibility in assignment so that managers can be moved to positions in which their skills can best be used.

There are encouraging signs that a corps of professional managers is emerging in the state-local sector. Some jurisdictions have taken aggressive action to employ professionals with recognized management capability. The number and quality of educational programs in public administration and public affairs have increased in recent years. Schools of business administration offer programs on management in the public

INDEPENDENT CIVIL SERVICE COMMISSIONERS
FILL TOP MANAGEMENT POSITIONS

In 1972, the civil service director forwarded the names of three finalists for the position of community development director to the city manager. This officer reported to the city manager, and therefore the latter could pick one of the three top candidates to fill the position. This list was determined as follows: The Civil Service Commission decided, following the recommendation of the civil service director, that an oral examination would be the sole basis for selection. Civil service technicians, none of whom had any managerial experience themselves, reviewed applications and narrowed the more than sixty candidates to eight. Why eight? Because there are eight hours in a working day, and the civil service director had allotted one day for conducting oral examinations.

The city manager was permitted to suggest questions to be asked in the oral interviews, but the civil service director determined the final questions. The civil service director then selected three people to comprise an oral examination board: the director of community development from a neighboring city, a professor of urban studies from Detroit, and a professor of land-use planning from Michigan State University. None of the three was a resident of Flint, knew much about the city and its particular community development needs, or knew anything about the management needs of the Department of Community Development.

Forty-five-minute interviews were held with each candidate. At the completion of the examination, each oral board member assigned points to each candidate, using a number of criteria in the scoring system developed by the Civil Service Commission. The three top scores for this position were 93.96, 93.61, and 80.96. The city manager had to choose one of the top three candidates. He chose the top scorer, who was, by civil service standards, the best candidate—by .35 of 1 percent.

Source: Brian W. Rapp and Frank M. Patitucci, *Managing Local Government for Improved Performance* (Boulder, Colo.: Westview Press, 1977), p. 65.

sector, and some schools have developed curricula that recognize the inherent similarities in management of large and complex organizations whether in the public or in the private sector.

There is, in fact, more available management talent than state and local governments are willing to employ. Part of the problem lies in the salaries that are offered for key positions. Whereas salaries for non-managerial positions tend to compare favorably with salaries for comparable positions in industry and the federal government, salaries for managerial posts tend to lag. Because the salaries of some top managers are noncompetitive, some of the best people, even those trained for the public service, continue to look to business or the federal government for employment. **Legislative bodies should ensure that compensation of top management and staff positions in the nation's large state, county, and city governments is competitive with that of similar positions in the private sector and the federal government.** It should be emphasized that we are not suggesting that state and local governments should attempt to compete with federal salaries for all positions, especially given the evidence of inflated federal compensation in middle management positions. We intend our recommendations to apply to the top managerial ranks only.

Even the best managers require opportunities for continual training and personal development. The private sector has long recognized the high return on investment in people, particularly in its management ranks, but state and local governments have little tradition of executive development programs to make the most of the managers they employ. **We recommend that state and local governments adopt specific policies for the continual training and development of their managers, establish their own programs or access to programs elsewhere, and appropriate specific funds for this purpose.** There seem to be particular gaps in managers' knowledge of employee relations, including both formal aspects of contract management and more subjective questions of day-to-day working relationships. Even those few governments that provide effective executive development opportunities tend to cut back funds for training during periods of fiscal stringency. Such tendencies are counterproductive and should be resisted.

We also encourage schools of management and public policy to recognize the growing importance of personnel management in making complex organizations function effectively and to strengthen their research and training in the legal, political, economic, managerial, and ethical aspects of personnel management and employee relations.

AUTHORITY AND RESOURCES TO MANAGE

Support from the top and adequate personnel are a government manager's most important assets. However, even the most capable managers who have these assets will be handicapped by rigid laws and restrictive procedures that impede the effective management of personnel. Many public managers must deal with complexity and constraints more formidable than any found in most business organizations. This is partly to be expected because of the political nature of government. Nonetheless, the constraints on most governments are unnecessarily paralyzing. Personnel regulations designed to meet the problems of an earlier age are seldom pruned when they have outlived their usefulness. Controls established to guard against political favoritism and graft now pose the equally ominous danger of crippling public-service operations. **In larger governments, the manager of an agency, department, or division should have principal responsibility for personnel matters in his or her unit. The head of the unit should be given reasonable authority to recruit, hire, train, assign, promote, discipline, adjust pay, and terminate employees under his or her control, with appropriate specialized support and with the guidance and control of government-wide personnel standards established by the central personnel office to assure the application of merit principles and protection of employees.** *

We caution elected officials not to expect their managers to exercise greater authority than they have been delegated from the top. If top policy makers cannot reach accord themselves on the direction of policy or the general means of implementation in line agencies, or if they are not willing to support professional managers on questions of policy and personnel behavior, it is unreasonable to expect managers to develop such authority on their own. The political nature of government is such that without clear direction from top political authorities, the focus on political forces will be shifted to the agencies and will complicate the job of the managers who run them.

It is current practice in most governments to absorb all improvements in efficiency or cost savings back into the general budget or to regard funds overtly or covertly set aside for management improvements as slush funds that will be aggressively sought out by budget examiners and pruned by legislators more concerned with the favorable publicity that attends budget cuts than with long-term improvement. This leaves managers with inadequate resources to invest in agency improvement. Some hide contingency funds in padded budgets and at year's end

*See memorandum by CHARLES P. BOWEN, JR., page 128.

wastefully spend the money rather than acknowledge it as a surplus. Consequently, systematic improvements in operations, which of course entail costs, are rarely undertaken, even though money may be available to do so. **Managers should be permitted and encouraged to establish separate and identifiable funds for continual analysis, experimentation, and improvement of their operations.**

As discussed in Chapter 4, collective bargaining increasingly involves matters that bear directly on the management of public services, including work load, staffing, assignment of personnel, productivity improvement, and incentive payment plans. Such matters cannot be considered in isolation by labor relations personnel and should be subject to review by operating managers. **In those jurisdictions that have collective bargaining, agency heads should play a role in bargaining with employees under their direction through formal and informal consultation with management's collective bargaining team.**

INCENTIVE TO MANAGE

If managers are to be given greater authority to run their agencies, they must also be held more strictly accountable for results. This can be accomplished through several approaches.

The development of a professional managerial corps should help to foster a tradition of greater managerial responsibility in the public sector, a tradition that should, in turn, encourage higher-quality management. To some extent, greater incentives for excellence in management should derive from a sense of dedication to professional standards and values inculcated in training, from a sense of allegiance to the profession in general and professional peers in particular, and from a sense of duty to public service.

A more tangible incentive is the recognition that career opportunities and advancement will depend upon demonstrated performance. As government officials seek qualified managers from outside government to head key agencies, selection and hence career advancement will depend increasingly upon demonstrated competence and performance; this is already the case in the city management profession. The better paid and more respected professional managers are, the greater the incentive to maintain good standing within the profession will be. The experience of the city management profession in building a sense of professional competence and responsibility, based largely on these factors, is evidence that this can be accomplished.

Assessing managerial performance requires being able to assess agency performance. Techniques of measurement and evaluation, systems for using them in operation, and the personnel to do evaluations are available. Systematic performance evaluation of government operations by departmental personnel, budget and management analysts, audit agencies, and legislative bodies constitutes one of the most hopeful means of assisting management and of holding managers accountable for the costs and results of government operations. **Governments should establish measures of performance and the capability for performance evaluation that are linked to the responsibilities and performance of individual managers through the budget, accounting procedures, or information systems.**

There are, of course, instances in which department heads or other nonelected officials acquire power of their own that derives from statutory authority, civil service protection, extreme loyalty of employees, or independent bases of power within the community. Such power can unduly insulate them from the direction of politically accountable officials. With few exceptions, however, that power could be overcome by the combined weight and determination of elected officials to secure appropriate changes in law that would restore an adequate measure of authority or to bring direct pressure to bear to gain compliance with duly established policy.

If managers are to be held accountable for unsatisfactory performance, they should also be rewarded for superior performance. **Management compensation should be more closely tied to performance. Specifically, we favor flexibility in law and regulation to reward significantly better-than-average performance with cash bonuses, as is the practice in private industry.**

SENIOR EXECUTIVE SERVICE

In order to develop a highly trained, experienced, and motivated corps of top public executives, several governments have established senior executive services made up of their top managers. The state of California has had such an arrangement for several years, and the states of Oregon and Minnesota have undertaken similar plans (see "Incentives and Performance: Minnesota's Management Plan," p. 99). At the federal level, the President has proposed to Congress that a senior executive service be created in the federal civil service for the top 9,000 managers in the GS supergrades 16, 17, and 18. Its purpose would be to increase incentive among managers in the federal government and provide top policy makers with greater latitude in using the skills of career managers in positions for which they are most capable or compatible.

In *Revitalizing the Federal Personnel System* (1978), this Committee recommended provisions for a senior executive service in the federal government that may also be applicable to the larger states and local governments. Its major provisions include the following:

- appointment to the senior executive service by an impartial qualifications board

- limits on the number of noncareer appointments to 10 or 15 percent of total professional executives

- assignment to any suitable post within the government at the discretion of appointing authorities

- discretion in the setting of salaries, with provision for bonuses for outstanding performance

- removal from a position or termination by an agency for any cause without the right of appeal but with the right of appointment to other agencies and with income security for one year following removal

We emphasize that there is still relatively little experience with such provisions for encouraging professional management in government. The experiences of the state governments that have tried them have been mixed, although on balance, they seem to be positive. Careful consideration must be exercised in their adoption, and provision must be made to monitor their actual effects in a way that takes into account variable state and local government settings.

MIDDLE MANAGEMENT AND SUPERVISORS

Middle-level management and first-line supervision constitute the critical link between top-level policy and implementation. Yet, it is precisely in this critical link that many governments face a crisis. Division managers and supervisors confront hostile and confusing forces: am-

INCENTIVES AND PERFORMANCE:

Minnesota's Management Plan

In an effort to establish a strong executive managerial team, Minnesota officials initiated a new management plan in 1976 covering approximately 400 senior state government managers. The plan defines management positions and responsibilities, bases pay adjustments exclusively on performance, allows managers to select from an array of fringe benefit options, and encourages management development. No manager is permitted to be a member of a collective bargaining unit.

A number of actions have been taken which Minnesota officials believe are necessary in establishing an eminently qualified managerial group in state government: (1) compensation has been linked directly to the state management by objective system, (2) longevity and seniority have been eliminated as the primary determinants of salary adjustments, and (3) fringe benefits have been tailored to the unique needs of individual managers. Yet, the management plan was never fully implemented as originally drawn. Formal management development courses have been temporarily abandoned. More significantly, six months after implementation, major changes were announced regarding compensation which effectively eliminated salary increases for many of the managers. Later changes rescinded the salary freeze.

Despite problems in implementation, modifications in the plan seem not to have caused irreparable damage. Results of a survey of the managers indicate the management plan was soundly conceived, and managers would like the plan continued in one form or another.

Source: James E. Jarret and Dick Howard, Council of State Governments, "Incentives and Performance: Minnesota's Management Plan," *Innovations* (February 1978): 1.

biguous and often conflicting direction from above, abuse from the public, media scrutiny, intrusions of reorganization and management fads, probing budget analysts, meddling management analysts, auditors and outside consultants, new regulations, public employment programs for special categories of workers, challenges from equal opportunity groups, workers who are perceived to be unreliable and disrespectful, and unions that seem to reinforce the intransigence of employees.

As the lines between labor and management in government are more sharply drawn, supervisors feel increasingly isolated. They are not fully accepted by either side. Most supervisors have been promoted to their positions from entry-level jobs and hence continue to feel a camaraderie with the employees who were formerly their companions. Top management may attempt to discourage this affinity and encourage supervisors to think of themselves as management; yet, often, they are not treated as such by top officials.

Employees promoted to supervisory or middle management jobs are rarely given adequate training to equip them for the substantially different responsibilities they will shoulder. They are thus not only psychologically and organizationally isolated but also professionally ill-equipped to handle the formidable burden of guiding a group of diverse employees in the execution of ambiguous policy encumbered with complex regulations in a politically charged atmosphere.

We believe it is of the utmost importance that governments recognize the plight of their middle-level managers and first-line supervisors and take steps to strengthen this critical group of government employees. **Promotion policy should place greater emphasis on identifying people with clear potential for supervisory and managerial positions and should de-emphasize seniority, written examinations, and narrow technical proficiencies that bear little relevance to future job responsibilities.** Greater reliance should be placed on personal evaluation of performance and potential by superiors, based on observation, evaluation against specific criteria of leadership potential, and use of performance assessment techniques that test capabilities relevant to supervision, judgment, and decision making.

We urge that training be provided for supervisors upon appointment and that they be given educational opportunity throughout their careers. This training and education should cover the principles and practice of supervision, basic and new management systems and techniques, labor relations, and the fundamentals of work measurement and performance evaluation. Efforts to improve productivity through the use

Figure 7: Attitudes toward Supervisors (percent)

Questions	Responses			
	Managers		Employees	
	Public Sector	Private Sector	Public Sector	Private Sector
All in all, how good a job is being done by your immediate supervisor (*% good*)	69.8	73.3	54.5	67.1
All in all, how good a job is being done by your supervisor's supervisor (*% good*)	54.6	63.7	42.6	55.9
My supervisor is competent technically/ knows the job (*% agree*)	73.3	80.4	65.0	79.6
My supervisor is competent in human relations/ dealing with the people who work for him/her (*% agree*)	67.3	63.0	52.7	61.2
How do you feel about the amount of emphasis on correcting poor employee performance in your organization (*% too little*)	(52.2) [a]	(30.0)	(49.4)	(36.6)

[a] Percentages in parentheses signify a negatively directed response; that is, the higher the percentage, the *less* favorable the indicated result.

Source: National Center for Productivity and Quality of Working Life, *Employee Attitudes and Productivity Differences Between the Public and Private Sector* (Washington, D.C., February 1978), pp. 10, 12.

of work standards often flounder because of lack of understanding and suspicion on the part of supervisors. The training required in many instances is in fundamentals of organizational design and operation, including budget making, accounting, work scheduling, contract administration, handling employee grievances, and nurturing positive employee relations, rather than in the finer points of management. (See Figure 7.)

If supervisors are to be considered part of management and are to feel themselves to be so, they should be excluded from bargaining units. Permitting supervisors to bargain and, especially, including supervisors in bargaining units with their subordinates not only confuses the relationship between supervisors and subordinates but also risks paralyzing government's ability to deal with labor disputes, slowdowns, and strikes. Middle-level managers and supervisors should be considered part of management, dealt with as management, and encouraged to think of themselves as such.

Chapter 6

EMPLOYEE PERFORMANCE AND SATISFACTION

INDIVIDUAL PERFORMANCE requires direction, ability, and motivation. Employees need to know what is expected of them. Even employees whose jobs require a high degree of self-direction or who are personally inclined to define their own work responsibly require definition of their objectives and the standards by which their work will be evaluated. In government, where overall goals are especially difficult to define, establishing clear and meaningful objectives for individual employees is a challenging task, but the challenge must be met. Establishment of objectives is a crucial first step in moving toward higher performance and a crucial last step in evaluating performance and providing feedback to employees on how well they are doing their jobs.

The level of employee ability is determined in the first instance by the effectiveness of procedures for recruiting, selecting, and assigning personnel and by the compensation offered to attract qualified people. Training that is geared specifically to the job to be performed, whether provided on the job or through formal prior instruction, is often required to translate personal potential into usable skills.

Motivating employees is increasingly challenging for several reasons. Wages, benefits, hours of work, and working conditions have always been the most important features of job motivation and satisfaction, the sine qua non of the quality of working life. However, as income levels have increased, hours of work have declined, and working conditions have improved, other objectives and higher-level employee needs have increased in relative importance. These higher needs include acceptance by peers and superiors, recognition of accomplishment, a sense of achievement, interest and stimulation in the job, advancement within the organization, a sense of participation, and opportunity for personal growth and meaningful use of one's abilities (variously called *individuation*, *self-actualization*, or *fulfillment*).

Labor organizations in Western industrial nations outside the United States have supported greater employee participation in management and greater attention to improving the quality of working life in support of higher individual goals. Although American industrial labor unions generally have not shown as much enthusiasm for such notions as industrial democracy, as practiced in Sweden and Germany, suspecting that they contain undercurrents of management manipulation, some American labor leaders in the public sector have suggested that greater employee participation and emphasis on the quality of working life could benefit employees and the effectiveness of public services. Reactions among managers have varied. Some have supported a greater emphasis on improving the quality of working life and employee participation as a means of increasing performance or humanizing work; others have rejected such notions as impediments to organizational performance.

Ideally, individual performance and satisfaction should be mutually reinforcing. Managers who can successfully blend individual goals with the broader purposes of their organization are likely to achieve higher performance, which, in turn, is an integral part of a satisfying work environment. However, performance and satisfaction can also be at odds with one another. The search for modes of operation that accommodate changing personal preferences is desirable, but it cannot be permitted to impede the fundamental purpose of government, which is to meet public needs effectively and efficiently.

Achieving higher employee performance and satisfaction depends upon a combination of financial and nonfinancial factors.

Figure 8: Comparative Levels
of Public and Private Compensation

Year	Private Sector	Federal Civilian Work Force	State and Local Government
Average wages and salaries per full-time equivalent employee			
1962	$ 5,082	$ 6,239	$ 5,017
1972	8,590	12,676	8,916
1975	10,690	15,195	10,862
1976	11,486	16,201	11,572
Average annual supplements to wage and salary per full-time equivalent employee			
1962	482	—	431
1972	1,150	1,497	1,110
1975	1,706	2,442	1,619
1976	1,904	2,809	1,848
Total compensation per full-time equivalent employee			
1962	5,564	—	5,448
1972	9,740	14,173	10,026
1975	12,396	17,637	12,481
1976	13,390	19,010	13,420

Source: Roy Bahl, Bernard Jump, and Larry Schroeder, "The Outlook for City Fiscal Performance in Declining Regions," *The Fiscal Outlook for Cities, Implications of a National Urban Policy,* ed., Roy Bahl (Syracuse, N.Y.: Syracuse University Press, 1978), table 11.

FINANCIAL COMPENSATION

Traditionally, government pay was determined almost exclusively by market factors; wages were set at the minimum level required to attract qualified people to perform public services. These comparatively low public wages were justified on the grounds that public employment offered greater job security, better working conditions, less pressure to perform, and the satisfaction of public service.

However, since World War II, the wages of public employees have improved significantly. By 1972, average state and local government wages had actually surpassed average private-sector wages. Since 1972, that advantage has diminished (see Figure 8). Between 1973 and 1975, both public-sector and private-sector workers experienced an average decline in real wages (see Figure 9), and the decline for public employees was slightly greater. From 1975 to 1976, average private wages continued to grow at a slightly higher rate than average public wages.

Of course, average wage figures tell a limited story. They do not distinguish among jurisdictions, occupational classes, or types of jobs.[1] As the data in Figure 10 demonstrate, government has a higher proportion of professional and technical personnel who generally command higher salaries. Federal government salaries, which on the average are significantly higher than either private-sector or state and local government salaries, in part reflect the larger number of professional and technical personnel in the federal service (although there is increasing concern about the overall level of federal salaries and benefits below the senior management ranks).[2]

Government wage levels have risen mainly to attract the large numbers of qualified people required to provide expanding public services (see Figure 11). Other contributing factors include growing political strength of public employees and their organizations, rising federal

---

1. A 1976 Bureau of Labor Statistics survey of public and private wages in twenty-four cities determined that clerical and custodial workers generally earned salaries comparable to those paid for similar jobs by the federal government and above those paid by private industry. Skilled maintenance workers had salaries below those paid for comparable jobs by the federal government and private industry. Charles Field V and Richard L. Keller, "How Salaries of Large Cities Compare with Industry and Federal Pay," *Monthly Labor Review* (November 1976): 23.

2. Jerome M. Rosow, "Public Sector Pay and Benefits," *Public Administration Review* (September-October 1976): 538-543.

Figure 9: Growth in the Cost of Employment in
the Public and Private Sectors (percent)

Year	All Industry	Private Industry	Federal Civilian	State and Local Government
Growth in wages and salaries per 1 percent increase in CPI[a]				
1962-1972	1.70	1.60	2.20	1.80
1972-1973	0.98	0.97	1.05	1.06
1973-1974	0.68	0.73	0.42	0.54
1974-1975	0.93	0.96	0.85	0.87
1975-1976	1.24	1.28	1.14	1.12
Growth in average annual supplements per 1 percent increase in CPI[a]				
1962-1972	2.8	2.8	—	3.0
1972-1973	2.5	2.5	2.1	2.0
1973-1974	1.1	1.1	1.7	1.4
1974-1975	1.6	1.6	2.3	1.4
1975-1976	2.1	2.0	2.6	2.4

[a]Consumer price index.
Source: Bahl, Jump, and Schroeder, "The Outlook for City Fiscal Performance in Declining Regions," table 14.

wages, federal and state grant programs, acceptance of built-in inflationary adjustments, and lax standards of so-called merit step increases.

Wages theoretically reflect the marginal contribution of labor to the value of the final product or service. However, in any large organization in which numerous individuals work together to produce a product or service, it is difficult, if not impossible, to determine the precise value of each individual's contribution. In the private sector, where products and services are valued according to market sales, a relationship may be established between the wages paid labor in general and the dollar value of final output. In government, where it is difficult to establish a dollar value of final output, establishing such a relationship is nearly impossible.

In order to pay wages that are both competitive and fair, many governments attempt to set their wages at levels that are comparable to similar jobs in the private sector. Although the comparability principle is a useful general measure for setting wages, it has shortcomings: It is difficult to find completely comparable jobs in government and business. Data collection is less than precise. And to the extent that government wages are in fact comparable to private wages, they will reflect whatever market distortions are present in private wages; for example, inflationary tendencies in private wages will be transferred to government wages.

Government wage rates are also determined by the ability of the government to pay. Ability to pay depends upon the tax base, access to revenues from other levels of government, restrictions on taxing authority (which is especially critical for local governments, whose taxing authority is determined by the state), borrowing power, and willingness of the public to be taxed.

Within the general constraints established by the competitive labor market and the ability to pay, government wages are determined by political factors. Policy makers judge what level and quality of employees they are willing to pay for and, in jurisdictions in which there is bargaining with employees, what they are willing to pay to maintain labor peace. The price of labor peace depends, in turn, partly upon the power and willingness of public employees to push for higher wages and partly upon the willingness of the public to withstand labor pressure, which may take the form of strikes or other disruptions of public services, in order to avoid paying higher wages that may be translated into higher taxes. In the end, setting wages for government jobs requires political judgment and negotiation.

We support the general principle that public-sector compensation should be equivalent to comparable jobs in other governments and in the private sector. However, we believe that the comparability principle should be applied with flexibility to take into account the economic and political differences among jurisdictions and the difficulty of establishing true comparability among jobs. Comparability should be viewed as only

Figure 10: Employment in Government and Private Industry, by Occupation, 1976 (percent)

Occupation	Government [a]	Private Industry
Total	100	100
White-collar workers	68	46
Professional and technical	36	11
Managers and administrators	8	10
Clerical	24	18
Sales	[b]	7
Blue-collar workers	14	39
Craft and related workers	6	14
Transport equipment operatives	3	4
Other equipment operatives	1	15
Nonfarm laborers	4	6
Service workers	18	13
Farm workers	[b]	2

Note: Because of rounding, sums of individual items may not equal totals.

[a] Excludes federal employment overseas.

[b] Less than 0.5 percent.

Source: U.S. Department of Labor, Bureau of Labor Statistics, *Government Occupations,* Bulletin 1955-42 (Washington, D.C.: U.S. Government Printing Office, 1978), p. 3.

one of many factors that enter into negotiations, not as the base from which bargaining proceeds.

Benefits

Setting financial compensation for public jobs is further complicated by the growing importance of benefits as a form of compensation. Although average real wages for state and local employees declined between 1973 and 1975, the real value of benefits increased an estimated 2.8 percent during the same period.

Few state and local governments calculate the value of employee benefits when determining the comparability of compensation with similar jobs in the private sector. And estimates of the value of compensation vary. One survey in 1975 found that in municipalities with a population over 10,000 (777, or 34 percent of all municipalities over 10,000 responded to the survey), the cost of providing benefits represented 46.4 percent of pay for hours worked for police and fire personnel and 41.0 percent of pay for hours worked for general government employees.[3] In the same year, industry employees received benefits equivalent to 39.8 percent of pay for hours worked.[4] Because most governments do not fully fund their pensions, the survey estimated that real pension costs are understated by 3 to 6 percent of total hours worked.[5] (See Figure 12.)

Many state and local governments are not aware of the full costs of the benefit programs they provide for their employees. Through oversight or conscious desire to hide the true costs of employee compensation, many governments have incurred debts or otherwise provided benefits without fully accounting for their impact on current and future tax burdens or, consequently, for their implications for financial solvency and credit ratings in capital markets. According to one estimate, the unfunded liability for state and local government pension systems in 1976

---

3. Edward H. Friend and Albert Pike 3d, *Third National Survey of Employee Benefits for Full-Time Personnel of U.S. Municipalities* (Washington, D.C.: Labor-Management Relations Service, U.S. Conference of Mayors, 1977), p. 3.

4. Friend and Pike, *Third National Survey of Employee Benefits for Full-Time Personnel of U.S. Municipalities*, p. 3. Hours worked does not include vacation, holidays, sick leave, and personal time such as lunch breaks. The figures are not totally comparable because the benefit figures for public employees represent payments by governments for employee benefits in that year, as opposed to the value of benefits, current and future, actually paid or obligated to employees in that year.

5. Friend and Pike, *Third National Survey of Employee Benefits for Full-Time Personnel of U.S. Municipalities*, p. 6. The concept of benefits and the methods for their calculation are far from uniform. The Urban Institute is currently engaged in a study to develop more precise measures of public-sector benefits. See, for example, Harold A. Hovey and Elizabeth Dickson, *Comparing Compensation in Major American Cities: Study Methodology* (Washington, D.C.: Urban Institute, March 15, 1978).

Figure 11: Attitudes toward Pay (percent)

Questions	Responses			
	Managers		Employees	
	Public Sector	Private Sector	Public Sector	Private Sector
How would you rate your pay compared to what you could get in other organizations you know about (% *good*)	47.3	35.0	30.6	32.6
How would you rate your pay considering your duties and responsibilities (% *good*)	31.9	25.4	30.5	26.1
All in all, I am satisfied with our benefits package (% *agree*)	73.1	70.1	64.3	68.7

Source: National Center for Productivity and Quality of Working Life, *Employee Attitudes and Productivity Differences Between the Public and Private Sector* (Washington, D.C., February 1978), p.15.

was approximately $270 billion.[6] For those governments that bargain collectively with employees, the temptation is especially great to hide employee gains won at the bargaining table in benefit packages that are never made intelligible to the public. Furthermore, many benefits come in terms of time off (sick leave, vacation, shorter workday, washup time, holidays, and the like). Therefore, comparisons among jurisdictions and

---

6. Alicia H. Munnell and Ann M. Connolly, "Funding Government Pensions: State-Local, Civil Service and Military," *Funding Pensions: Issues and Implications for Financial Markets*, Conference Series no. 16 (Boston: Federal Reserve Bank of Boston, 1976), p. 73.

between the public and the private employer should be on the basis of total compensation per hour worked. **We strongly recommend that the total costs of employee benefits be fully calculated for both current and future years and that comparability of compensation with the private sector or other governments be established on the basis of total compensation, including benefits as well as wages and salaries.**

Compensation for work comprises a multitude of factors, including wages, financial benefits, nonfinancial benefits such as time off, job security, working conditions, and opportunities for personal growth and career advancement. The factors that constitute the compensation package can have quite different values to different groups of employees and to different individuals. Older workers, for example, tend to place greater value on retirement benefits; whereas younger workers are more interested in raising current income. Employees in higher tax brackets may prefer nontaxable benefits to salary increases; many people would prefer additional time off to comparable increases in salary. **We urge governments to be more discriminating in tailoring compensation packages to the needs and desires of groups of employees and to individuals. Greater attention to the marginal value of each component of compensation could produce greater value to the employee for the same compensation or the same value to employees at lower aggregate cost to the government.**

In recent years, widespread attention has been given to the costs of meeting pension obligations, the tendency toward early retirement or questionable disability retirement in the police and fire services, and the underfunding of pension systems. Nevertheless, the dangers of excessive pension obligations still go unheeded by most local governments. **We urge state governments to examine the benefit systems, especially pensions, of their local governments to assure that all costs are clearly stated and that pension systems are based on sound, well-understood actuarial principles (if not necessarily fully funded).** In some instances, it may be desirable for states to take a more direct role in the regulation or management of local government benefit systems. But in all cases, state governments should be aware that insolvency or fiscal mismanagement by local governments can lead to state burdens. Prudent action by state governments is indicated.

In *Improving Productivity in State and Local Government,* we urged states to facilitate the portability of pensions among governments in order to permit a higher degree of mobility for public employees. We reiterate our support of that recommendation. We further urge consideration of joint intergovernmental pension funds for management-level personnel to facilitate their mobility.

One of the major impediments to effective state and local government compensation policy is inadequate information. There is no comprehensive, reliable, and regularly gathered information on wages and benefits of state and local government employees. The Bureau of Labor Statistics has begun to undertake individual city wage surveys on an ad hoc basis; this information is useful but far from sufficient. **We strongly urge the Bureau of Labor Statistics, the Office of Management and Budget, and Congress to allocate the resources required to provide data on public employment, including data for both wages and benefits, that are at least equivalent to those provided on private employment.**

Pay as Incentive for Performance

Current pay systems assume that employees are doing their jobs satisfactorily and hence deserve their pay unless there is clear evidence to the contrary. Periodic step increases in pay are given as a right of seniority rather than as a reward for performance. Such practices tend to undermine morale among productive employees, dull the desire to perform, and constitute a further burden on government budgets. Two employees in the same job classification should not earn the same wage when one clearly outperforms the other and contributes far more to the organization. We are sympathetic with the concern that performace evaluation invites arbitrariness, racial and sexual discrimination, favoritism, and political abuse. However, we reject the notion that merit should be defined as the ability to meet minimum standards, rather than as exceptional performance. Managers should be given latitude to reward superior performers.

The public sector generally has not taken advantage of financial incentives to promote productivity, partly because of the difficulty of establishing measurable performance targets that can serve as a basis for evaluating performance and tying those targets to financial reward. However, increasing interest in and growing experimentation with financial incentive programs suggest that there is greater potential than may have been recognized.[7] **We urge further experimentation with**

---

7. John M. Greiner et al., "Monetary Incentives for State and Local Government Employees: An Examination of Current Usage, Impacts, and Implementation Factors" (Washington, D.C.: Urban Institute, 1977).

Figure 12: Composite Employee Benefit Component Expenditures

Type of Employee Benefit	Sworn Personnel [a]	
	Percent of Pay for Hours Worked	Cents per Hour Worked
Pension and social security	14.74	74.7¢
Paid vacations	6.72	34.1
Health benefits	3.75	19.4
Workmen's compensation	2.79	14.5
Paid sick leave	2.73	14.0
Death benefits	0.67	3.5
Holidays	4.74	24.2
Long-term disability benefits	0.22	1.1
Unemployment compensation	0.03	0.1
Uniforms	1.78	9.0
Military training time	0.09	0.5
Nonproduction bonuses	1.32	6.7
Paid jury duty	0.29	1.6
Educational expense	0.43	2.2
Personal time-expense allowance	6.07	31.5
Total	46.37	237.1¢

[a]Uniformed police officers and fire fighters.

Source: Edward H. Friend and Albert Pike 3d, *Third National Survey of Employee Benefits for Full-Time Personnel of U.S. Municipalities* (Washington, D.C.: Labor-Management Relations Service, U.S. Conference of Mayors, 1977), p. 6.

financial incentive programs to improve performance. **Emphasis should be placed on financial bonuses that reflect specific and measurable increases in performance, rather than on permanent salary increases that may perpetuate financial rewards even though productivity may**

Sworn Personnel[a]		General Personnel			
Dollars per Year	Percent	Percent of Pay for Hours Worked	Cents per Hour Worked	Dollars per Year	Percent
$1,557	32	13.13	57.5¢	$1,090	32
710	14	4.75	20.9	396	12
399	8	4.46	19.7	373	11
302	6	2.89	12.4	237	7
291	6	2.75	12.2	230	7
69	1	0.51	2.2	42	1
497	10	3.99	17.6	333	10
23	1	0.25	1.0	19	1
3	0	0.04	0.2	3	0
184	4	1.06	4.3	83	2
9	0	0.06	0.3	5	0
140	3	0.42	1.7	32	1
31	1	0.07	0.3	5	0
46	1	0.10	0.4	8	0
646	13	6.48	28.2	536	16
$4,907	100	40.96	178.9¢	$3,392	100

decline. Such programs should be accompanied by carefully designed program evaluation to monitor their effects on productivity, employee satisfaction, and labor-management relations.

In some states, financial incentive programs are effectively prohibited by law. **We recommend that state legislatures remove barriers** and otherwise explicitly permit and encourage the use of incentives, including monetary incentive programs, to improve government performance.

Under current public pay systems, a superior employee who is at the top step in his or her grade can receive additional compensation only if he or she is promoted to the next-highest grade. Some employees may take a promotion and change jobs in order to get the additional pay even though they would prefer to stay in their old job. They may be unsuited for the higher-level job or have little desire to perform in the new role. This problem is particularly acute for professional and technical personnel whose skills may be of equal or greater value to the organization than those of administrators but who are forced to take administrative jobs in order to increase their salaries. In business, it is not unusual to find highly paid specialists who make more than their management superiors; in many cases, they prefer not to leave their technical positions, and the firms recognize their value in their current jobs. **We believe that public pay systems should have the flexibility to give higher pay to valuable professional and technical personnel, even if it exceeds the pay of their management superiors. Such personnel, whose contributions are clearly important to the agency, should not be forced, as they currently are, to choose between stagnant wages and a promotion to an administrative job that they do not seek.**

Inadequate financial compensation can affect employee incentive negatively, but increases in compensation will not necessarily guarantee higher performance (except to eliminate a source of grievance that can lead to lower performance). Greater job satisfaction and incentives for improving performance increasingly derive from nonfinancial factors.

ROLE OF THE INDIVIDUAL IN THE ORGANIZATION

A personal sense of accomplishment depends in large measure on feeling that one is performing meaningful work that contributes to broader goals. If the organization has no clear sense of purpose or is perceived as being unproductive, its employees will tend to think of themselves in the same manner.[8]

---

8. See, for example, Katherine C. Janka, Robert A. Luke, and Charles A. Morrison, *People, Performance . . . Results: A Guide to Increasing the Effectiveness of Local*

Most governments are organized into departments according to traditional functions, such as police, health, and transportation. Yet, many of the problems faced by governments do not respect strict functional divisions. Thus, employees may find themselves bound by bureaucratic lines of authority to tasks that seem to have little to do with the real problems they face. For example, police officers know that the effectiveness of their efforts to apprehend criminals depends on the cooperation of the public, the assistance of crime victims, the competence of prosecuting attorneys, and the disposition of judges, but they also know that they are perceived by the public as being primarily accountable for law enforcement. Similarly, schoolteachers know that there is a limit to what they can accomplish with students whose families have given them little self-discipline and encouragement to learn.

People who lose sight of the meaning of their work or who feel that their actions show few results are inclined to consider their jobs solely as a means of generating income. Consequently, their performance is not only uninspired but may also be indifferent to the needs of the organization as a whole. For example, an ambulance driver who sees his job narrowly as driving a truck will probably do a poorer job and think less highly of himself than a driver who sees his job as helping to save lives.

EMPLOYEE PARTICIPATION

Employees are a prime but curiously underutilized source of information on how to improve public-service operations. To the extent that their active participation is sought, their understanding of policy will be enhanced, and their commitment to implementing it will be increased. Positions that require the exercise of discretion and professional judgment, such as police work, social work, and teaching, in fact require employees to interpret policy in the daily performance of their duties. To the extent that the sense of participation increases employee security, relieves fears, or satisfies a desire to be treated as a responsible adult, it may create the mutual trust and the desire to contribute that can enhance organizational performance.

Responses to opportunities for greater participation and self-definition of work vary from person to person. Those with imagination, skill,

Government Employees (Washington, D.C.: National Training and Development Service Press, 1977).

and determination may take the opportunity both to improve the work process and to create a more satisfying environment for themselves. Others may take advantage of the situation for their own gain and give little thought to the organizational consequences. Still others will be perplexed and seek direction. Attempts to involve employees more fully in advising or participating in decisions regarding modes of operation need to allow for differences among individuals.

Although greater employee participation may enhance some types of operations, it may impede others. For example, the overall organization and functioning of a fire department may benefit from the expertise of fire fighters in identifying ways to improve staffing schedules, deployment, technology, labor-managment relations, and the like, but the actual fighting of a fire requires a highly disciplined, strict command-and-control mode of operation.

It should be recalled that in government, employees have opportunities to influence policy making that are largely absent in the private sector. By voting, supporting candidates for office, and lobbying, either as individuals or in groups, public employees can have a significant impact on the goals and means of operation of government programs and personnel policy.

One method of increasing employee participation to improve operations is through labor-management committees designed to identify and implement ways of improving productivity and the quality of working life. (See "Labor-Management Committee in Springfield, Ohio," pages 120–121.) Because they are created to function outside the adversary environment of the formal collective bargaining process, such committees can explore cooperative means of improving productivity, employee working conditions, and the working relationships between managers and employees. **We urge management and employees to develop means outside the formal collective bargaining process for developing their common interest in promoting productivity and the quality of working life. These means should include, but not necessarily be limited to, labor-management committees.**

Collective bargaining is clearly a form of employee participation in decisions that can affect both policy and operations. But because it is an adversary procedure, it should, to the greatest extent possible, be confined to topics on which management and employees have natural adversary positions. Separate mechanisms should be established and relationships nurtured that emphasize their mutual interest in serving the public and building pride and satisfaction in their work.

NATURE OF THE JOB

Job design can also affect performance and satisfaction. Many employees fail to contribute their maximum and feel frustrated simply because their jobs lack clear and meaningful objectives and work standards. Of course, there will always be malingerers. But most people prefer to spend their days in meaningful pursuits and return home with a sense of having put in a good day's work rather than while away their working hours tediously watching the clock and strenuously devising surreptitious means of convincing co-workers and supervisor that they are engaged in productive work. A sense of individual accomplishment and a feeling of having contributed to a higher and worthwhile organizational purpose are probably the most important elements in both job satisfaction and personal productivity (see Figure 13).

Closely related to the sense of accomplishment is the belief that one has fully used his or her abilities in performing the job. Employees who are assigned to jobs that do not tap their skills or abilities become frustrated, enervated, and resentful. Supervisors can be impeded in assigning work or reassigning employees according to their abilities by rigid classification systems that define jobs too narrowly, by personnel restrictions that inhibit flexibility in work assignment, and by static and timid general organizational policy and style.

A number of approaches can be used to relieve monotony, increase job interest, provide stimulation, and more fully tap employee potential:

● *Job Enlargement.* Additional tasks can be added to those jobs that underutilize employee skills or time.

● *Job Enrichment.* Jobs can be redesigned to involve each employee more fully in a given organizational task rather than confining his or her role to only one small part of it in the traditional assembly-line fashion.

● *Job Rotation.* Employees can be moved from job to job to relieve monotony and increase familiarity with other parts of the operation so that each can do his or her job more effectively for having a better understanding of how it relates to the whole.

● *Broader and More Flexible Job Classification.* Formal civil service or personnel classifications can be restructured to permit supervisors greater flexibility in assigning work as required by changing agency objectives or work load.

LABOR-MANAGEMENT COMMITTEE
IN SPRINGFIELD, OHIO

Springfield, Ohio, a highly industrialized city of 85,000, with a vigorous union representing a large proportion of its 740 municipal workers, embarked on an unusual experiment in cooperative labor-management relations. First reports indicate that, while both sides continue to protect their own interests, they are beginning to work together to find ways to serve the city better and at the same time enhance their own job satisfaction.

[The Quality of Work Life Experiment involved a five-step operation spread over 42 months:]

1. Negotiation of a cooperative agreement in which the parties mutually endorse common assumptions and goals (e.g., that improving the quality of the working environment will benefit both worker well-being and productivity), and agree [to] a 42-month process of testing the assumptions and working toward the goals. This cooperative agreement is ratified by the union membership.

2. Creation of a 10-member top-level Quality of Work Committee with equal numbers from the city and union. Monthly meetings are held with agendas from both sides.

3. Administration of a comprehensive work attitude survey to groups of workers, 20 at a time, for two-hour periods. Some of the Springfield/ AFSCME results, which are now being fed back and discussed in each

● *Flexible Working Hours.* Jobs can be designed to allow employees flexibility tailored to their personal and work lives. Some organizations have experimented with Flextime, which permits workers greater flexibility in arranging their work schedules to fit their personal needs. Others have developed a variety of work schedules, including a growing emphasis on part-time work. Although there is little evidence that such plans have a marked positive effect on productivity, they do demonstrate that many types of work can be flexibly organized to accommodate a diversity of life-styles and personal needs without sacrificing performance.

group, were surprising to project leaders—workers were not as critical of first-line supervision as expected; there was a big desire for increased opportunities for growth, learning, and additional responsibility; there was also a big desire for resources and equipment to do their jobs, coupled with an understanding of budgetary constraints (supervisors had thought they were unaware and not necessarily interested).

4. Participation in exchanges of information and experiences with other innovative organizations throughout the country, as arranged by the Project Coordinator. The OQWP [Ohio Quality of Work Project] sponsors visits to cities or plants, seminars by work restructuring experts with city employees and twice-a-year conferences attended by rank and file workers as well as union and management officials. These conferences feature labor/management/worker panels from experimenting organizations both in and outside Ohio.

5. Development and implementation of a plan based on the survey-feedback process and the experiences of other experimenting organizations. This plan lays out in rather specific terms the Committee's plans to institutionalize quality of work improvement mechanisms. The plan is ratified by the union membership.

Source: Sam Zagoria, *Productivity—A Positive Route* (Washington, D.C.: Labor-Management Relations Service, U.S. Conference of Mayors, 1978), appendix 3, pp. 16 and 17.

PERSONAL DEVELOPMENT

In business, the importance and sensibleness of well-designed training programs can often be quantitatively documented; but in government, training costs are typically considered to be an overhead expense and pose a highly visible and vulnerable target in an agency budget. A survey by the International City Management Association found that in 1974, 75 percent of cities responding allocated less than $25,000 to employee training. Cities with populations over 100,000 typically spent no more than one-tenth of 1 percent of their budgets on training.[9] Lack of good means of evaluation to document the benefits of government training programs and evidence that some programs have little relation to real job preparation and performance reinforce the notion that money spent for training is often wasted. **We recommend that governments support employee training and education programs specifically tailored to both current job requirements and future job skills that anticipate emerging public-service needs.**

Government, like business, depends heavily on public and private education to train people for employment. There are increasing complaints in both the public and the private sector that schools are producing graduates who do not possess basic skills in reading, writing, and arithmetic and the self-discipline required to perform most jobs in the modern economy. **A first step toward better preparation for job performance in government—and in the private sector—is to improve the nation's elementary, secondary, and vocational schools and institutions of higher learning to assure that students are provided with basic skills and vocational and professional training that will prepare them for employment.**

Training programs for entry-level positions in government agencies tend to be deficient in providing employees with the skills required to perform the jobs for which they were hired, although there are important exceptions, such as the high-caliber training that is provided for sworn police and fire officers in some jurisdictions. Furthermore, in many government agencies, training for supervisory positions is nonexistent. Nor are there sufficient opportunities for professional, technical, and administrative personnel to get the training they need to keep up with rapid changes in their fields.

Personal growth and development depend not just on training but also on opportunities to develop potential on the job (see Figure 14). Private industry has long recognized that one of the most effective ways to develop personal talents is to give employees clear responsibility and performance targets; equip them with the necessary resources, including training where necessary; and hold them responsible for performing progressively more challenging assignments.

---

9. *The Municipal Yearbook 1976* (Washington, D.C.: International City Management Association, 1976), p. 188.

Figure 13: Attitudes toward Job Satisfaction (percent)

Questions	Responses			
	Managers		Employees	
	Public Sector	Private Sector	Public Sector	Private Sector
How do you rate your job itself—that is, the type of work you do (% good)	84.3	88.8	64.0	73.5
My job makes good use of my skills and abilities (% disagree)	(14.3) [a]	(19.0)	(22.6)	(28.2)
I am permitted to make the decisions necessary to do my job effectively (% agree)	66.5	72.7	52.2	60.1
All in all, my organization is an effectively managed, well-run organization (% agree)	45.2	52.5	28.2	43.5
How would you rate your organization on producing work of high quality (% good)	61.9	73.0	54.0	62.3

[a]Percentages in parentheses signify a negatively directed response; that is, the higher the percentage, the *less* favorable the indicated result.

Source: National Center for Productivity and Quality of Working Life, *Employee Attitudes and Productivity Differences Between the Public and Private Sector,* pp. 10, 11.

124

Figure 14: Attitudes toward Personal Development (percent)

Questions	Responses			
	Managers		Employees	
	Public Sector	Private Sector	Public Sector	Private Sector
The better my performance, the better will be my opportunity for promotion to a better job (% agree)	43.3	58.3	30.2	48.7
I receive enough feedback on how well I do my work (% agree)	45.3	41.5	30.0	48.5
I am satisfied with my advancement since starting work here (% agree)	55.7	48.6	29.3	38.0
I am satisfied with my opportunity to move to a better job (% agree)	24.4	35.6	19.0	22.9
I am satisfied with management's efforts to promote from within (% agree)	57.4	59.5	36.0	43.8

Source: National Center for Productivity and Quality of Working Life, *Employee Attitudes and Productivity Differences Between the Public and Private Sector,* pp. 15, 17.

Education does not—and should not—stop with the beginning of a wage-earning career. Rather, it should continue, formally and informally, throughout a person's active working life and beyond. Most current job structures and personnel systems not only fail to facilitate periodic or continued education but usually pose a severe obstacle to it. There should also be greater potential for flexibility in personal career choice. Changes in career patterns can allow individuals to develop new skills and find a sense of renewal and stimulation. An increased supply of people who have gained breadth of experience and the capability to synthesize knowledge from diverse fields of specialization can help to improve the operation of government. Public personnel policy should recognize that employees are people with full lives to lead.

Memoranda
of Comment, Reservation,
or Dissent

Page 11, by W. D. DANCE, *with which* CHARLES P. BOWEN, JR., *has asked to be associated*

This policy statement can make a valuable contribution to the deliberations of all who seek to improve the management of the public work force, and for that reason I approve its issuance. It is probably impossible, however, to endorse any statement of such scope without reservations about some of its premises and conclusions, which I have. I am especially concerned with the section on collective bargaining because the rise of membership, militancy, and direct political activity of public-employee unions has to date constituted the most formidable impediment to the intelligent and efficient management of the work force.

Pages 19 and 62, by WILLIAM F. MAY, *with which* CHARLES P. BOWEN, JR., *has asked to be associated*

The conclusions and recommendations in this paper regarding the labor relations problems between public-sector employees and management were developed with considerable difficulty and are rather neutral and general. In my opinion the Committee had an almost impossible task. Collective bargaining is a most effective procedure for the resolution of economic-related issues between independent parties in a market economy. It is, however, only applicable to situations involving independent parties with approximately equal economic power and where the resolution of the issues is of relatively equal benefit to the parties and the failure to resolve involves equal penalties to each. In the case of public-service organizations without profit performance demands and where the management's future job security is dependent in part upon the actions of their employees, the collective bargaining process has limited applications.

Pages 19 and 62, by ROBERT R. NATHAN

The right to organize and bargain collectively for employees in public service is a relatively recent phenomenon. For many years there were serious doubts about the feasibility, let alone the propriety, of government workers having the opportunity to organize themselves into unions and to bargain with governmental units. Over the past decade or more this issue has in part been resolved by the fact that many hundreds of thousands of government employees—federal, state, and local—have joined unions and do, legally as well as effectively, engage in collective bargaining.

The consequences have certainly not been catastrophic, as opponents warned. On the other hand, there have been instances of serious disruption of essential public services in the fields of education, health, law and order, and fire protection. It would be improper to conclude either that the damages have been severe and irreparable or that there has been no cost to the public. The cost primarily resulted from strikes rather than negotiating excessive pay levels or wasteful and costly work rules.

As with all such issues, the costs and benefits need to be balanced. In my judgment responsible collective bargaining will bring more benefits than costs. Government workers are as fully aware of their obligations to their fellow citizens as any other group in our society. Overwhelmingly, they have performed well and bargained responsibly. In fact, given the relatively modest increases in state and local wages during much of the 1970s, the record is one which would justify rather than condemn public employees' right to collective bargaining.

Recent widespread disruptions are attributable to the nearly un-manageable combination of severe inflation and a squeeze on govern-ment budgets. Given these circumstances, I would still say that collec-tive bargaining by public-service employees has been fruitful. It can yield more benefits to society than the many adverse consequences associated with the denial of the right of state and local government employees to organize and bargain collectively.

Pages 23 and 95, by CHARLES P. BOWEN, JR., *with which* EDWARD L. PALMER *has asked to be associated*

Although these government-wide personnel standards should cer-tainly not be violated, neither should they be used as an excuse for management's failure to take personnel actions required to improve the quality, timeliness, and cost of governmental services.

Citizens, whose taxes pay directly or indirectly for these services, are entitled to effective governmental managers. Such managers distinguish between (1) the imperative need to select competent employees and place them in productive organization structures and (2) the social responsibility and probable political necessity to provide inef-fective and unmotivated employees with jobs and compensation suited to their demonstrated talent but which do not impair the effectiveness of government services. It is not the fault of such employees that they have been overpromoted because of a personnel system that has consistently rewarded time served instead of performance. The cost of continuing such employees on the payroll until retraining, appropriate relocation, or removal by attrition is not an added cost. It is simply a newly recognized excess cost and an alternative to unemployment. Made in-evitable by prior poor management, this cost should be identified as such and be included in the budget of the unit that created the situation.

To the extent that retraining may help these employees be more useful and productive, so much the better. But statutes, regulations, or political pressures that prevent, impede, or delay the required manage-ment action are clearly not in the public interest.

Page 84, by W. D. DANCE, *with which* CHARLES P. BOWEN, JR., *has asked to be associated.*

I do not believe that the factors enumerated as favoring manage-ment in public-sector labor disputes (in the following several pages) balance, to any degree, the perils to safety and health or the gross inconvenience and economic burdens public-employee strikes have been shown to impose.

Appendix A: Public Expenditures in the United States as Percent of GNP, 1957 and 1977 (billions)[a]

	Amount[a]		Percent of GNP	
	1957	1977	1957	1977
GNP	$443	$1,890	100.0	100.0
Total government expenditures[b]	115	621	26.0	32.9
Federal	80	423	18.1	22.4
State and local	40	265	9.0	14.0
Components of federal expenditures[c]				
Purchases of goods and services	50	145	11.3	7.7
Defense	44	94	9.9	5.0
Nondefense	6	51	1.4	2.7
Transfers to persons	16	170	3.6	9.0
Grants to state and local governments	4	68	0.9	3.6
Components of state and local expenditures				
Purchases of goods and services	37	250	8.4	13.2
Transfers to persons	4	28	0.9	1.5

[a]Expressed in current dollars.

[b]Federal grants to state and local governments are included in the federal and the state and local expenditures, but the duplication is eliminated in the combined total.

[c]Omits several miscellaneous items.

Source: *Economic Report of the President* (Washington, D.C.: U.S. Government Printing Office, January 1978); U.S. Department of Commerce, Bureau of Economic Analysis, *Survey of Current Business* (Washington, D.C.: U.S. Government Printing Office, May 1978), tables 12 and 13, p. 9.

Appendix B: State and Local Government Employment, by Function, October 1976

Function	Full-Time Equivalent Employment	
	Number (thousands)	Percent
Total	10,206	100.0
Education	5,003	49.0
Local schools	3,862	37.8
Institutions of higher education	1,056	10.3
Other education	85	0.8
Hospitals	960	9.4
Highways	551	5.4
Police protection	546	5.4
Public welfare	342	3.4
General control	341	3.3
Financial administration	260	2.5
Local fire protection	215	2.1
Correction	206	2.0
Local utilities other than water supply[a]	190	1.9
Health	189	1.9
Natural resources	177	1.7
Local parks and recreation	149	1.5
Sanitation other than sewerage	121	1.2
Water supply	118	1.2
Employment security administration	103	1.0
Sewerage	82	0.8
All other	655	6.4

[a]Electric power, transit, and gas supply systems.

Source: U.S. Department of Commerce, Bureau of the Census, *Public Employment in 1976* (Washington, D.C.: U.S. Government Printing Office, 1977), p. 3.

Appendix C: Summary of State and Local Government

Function	State and Local Government	State Government	
Number of full-time employees who belong to an employee organization	4,736,962	991,634	
Education	2,637,217	236,837	
Teachers	2,059,784	96,752	
Other	577,433	140,085	
Highways	240,111	137,523	
Public welfare	138,102	61,497	
Hospitals	359,813	230,101	
Police protection	288,329	35,297	
Fire protection	150,507	—	
Sanitation other than sewerage	58,579	—	
All other functions	864,304	290,379	
Percent of full-time employees who belong to an employee organization	49.8%	38.2%	
Education	58.3	28.6	
Teachers	68.6	34.3	
Other	37.9	25.6	
Highways	44.3	53.5	
Public welfare	41.3	39.3	
Hospitals	39.5	47.7	
Police protection	54.3	51.8	
Fire protection	71.6	—	
Sanitation other than sewerage	49.2	—	
All other functions	36.9	36.2	

Source: U.S. Bureau of the Census, *Labor-Management Relations in State and Local Governments: 1976*.

Organized Employees, October 1976

Local Governments					
Total	Counties	Muni-cipalities	Townships	Special Districts	School Districts
3,745,328	502,163	1,075,727	124,208	119,035	1,924,195
2,400,380	151,836	247,054	77,295	—	1,924,195
1,963,032	134,961	200,279	63,702	—	1,564,090
437,348	16,875	46,775	13,593	—	360,105
102,588	38,596	52,499	9,762	1,731	—
76,605	54,574	21,931	100	—	—
129,712	59,716	55,817	401	13,778	—
253,032	43,745	194,904	14,383	—	—
150,507	7,851	136,493	5,360	803	—
58,579	2,396	52,751	3,354	78	—
573,925	143,449	314,278	13,553	102,645	—
54.1%	36.6%	53.5%	57.1%	37.3%	64.2%
64.9	56.7	74.4	78.7	—	64.2
72.1	67.2	78.1	84.6	—	71.5
44.8	25.2	61.9	59.2	—	44.4
36.0	30.8	43.1	29.5	38.2	—
43.0	39.8	55.3	8.1	—	—
30.3	28.9	48.4	37.0	13.1	—
54.7	43.1	57.9	59.2	—	—
71.6	56.3	75.5	64.6	11.4	—
49.2	27.8	50.3	68.0	12.4	—
37.3	28.2	40.2	29.3	50.0	—

State and Local Government Special Studies no. 88 (Washington, D.C.: U.S. Government Printing Office, 1978), p. 9.

Appendix D: State Policy Regarding Public-Employee Strikes, 1976		
State	*Coverage*	*Strike Policy*
Alaska	All public employees except teachers	Law enforcement, fire and hospital employees may not strike. They must resort to arbitration. Public safety, snow removal, sanitation and education employees may strike until there is a threat to public health, safety and welfare. All other employees may strike after majority vote.
Hawaii	All public employees	Prohibited unless impasse procedures have been complied with and 60 days have elapsed since fact-finding report was issued. Board may set requirements to avoid or remove danger to public health or safety. Board may seek injunctions for strikes in violation of these procedures.
Minnesota	All public employees	Prohibited. Employees may be terminated. Union decertified for two years, loses dues deduction privileges for two years. Employers' refusal to comply with an arbitration award or submit to arbitration is a defense against charges brought under this provision.
Montana	All public employees	Permitted.
	Nurses	Permitted upon 30 days notice provided there is no other strike at a health care facility within 150-mile radius.

State	Coverage	Strike Policy
	Appendix D: *(continued)*	
Oregon	All public employees except mass transit	Permitted after use of mediation and fact-finding provided 10 days notice is given and 30 days have elapsed since fact-finding report was made public. Employer may seek an injunction against strikes where there is a clear and present danger to the public health, safety or welfare. Strike in violation of injunction subjects union to fines. ULP [unfair labor practices] is not a defense to a prohibited strike. Employees may not strike unless they have an exclusive bargaining agent recognized by the employer or certified by the Board or where there is an interest arbitration provision. Employees other than those engaged in a nonprohibited strike who refuse to cross picket line are deemed to be engaged in a prohibited strike. Police, fire fighters and guards at prisons or mental hospitals may not strike.
Penn-sylvania	All public employees	Guards or court employees may not strike. Other employees may strike after mediation and fact-finding. Employer may seek injunction against illegal strikes or those presenting a clear and present danger to public health, safety or welfare. ULP not a defense to an illegal strike. Employees may not be paid for period of

Appendix D: *(continued)*

State	Coverage	Strike Policy
Penn-sylvania	All public employees	strike. Court may punish violation of injunction with fines or imprisonment. Employees other than those on strike who refuse to cross a picket line are deemed to be engaged in a prohibited strike.
Vermont	State employees	Prohibited. Employees may not recognize picket lines.
	Municipal employees	Strikes are not prohibited unless they occur within 30 days of issuance of fact-finding report, occur after parties have agreed to arbitration, or endanger public health, safety or welfare. Employer may seek an injunction where appropriate.
	Teachers	Prohibited. May be enjoined upon showing of clear and present danger.
Wisconsin	State employees	Prohibited. Employer may seek an injunction or file ULP charges or both. Employer may discipline strikers, cancel reemployment eligibility, request fines or damages from union.
	Municipal employees	Prohibited. Police must resort to arbitration. Strikers may be fined $10 per day.
	Police and fire fighters	Strikes and lockouts prohibited. Strikers may be fined $10 per day.

Appendix D: *(continued)*

Source: U.S. Department of Labor, Labor-Management Services Administration, *Summary of Public Sector Labor Relations Policies* (Washington, D.C.: U.S. Government Printing Office, 1976).

Objectives of the Committee for Economic Development

For thirty-five years, the Committee for Economic Development has been a respected influence on the formation of business and public policy. CED is devoted to these two objectives:

To develop, through objective research and informed discussion, findings and recommendations for private and public policy which will contribute to preserving and strengthening our free society, achieving steady economic growth at high employment and reasonably stable prices, increasing productivity and living standards, providing greater and more equal opportunity for every citizen, and improving the quality of life for all.

To bring about increasing understanding by present and future leaders in business, government, and education and among concerned citizens of the importance of these objectives and the ways in which they can be achieved.

CED's work is supported strictly by private voluntary contributions from business and industry, foundations, and individuals. It is independent, nonprofit, nonpartisan, and nonpolitical.

The two hundred trustees, who generally are presidents or board chairmen of corporations and presidents of universities, are chosen for their individual capacities rather than as representatives of any particular interests. By working with scholars, they unite business judgment and experience with scholarship in analyzing the issues and developing recommendations to resolve the economic problems that constantly arise in a dynamic and democratic society.

Through this business-academic partnership, CED endeavors to develop policy statements and other research materials that commend themselves as guides to public and business policy; for use as texts in college economics and political science courses and in management training courses; for consideration and discussion by newspaper and magazine editors, columnists, and commentators; and for distribution abroad to promote better understanding of the American economic system.

CED believes that by enabling businessmen to demonstrate constructively their concern for the general welfare, it is helping business to earn and maintain the national and community respect essential to the successful functioning of the free enterprise capitalist system.

Honorary Trustees

Trustees on Leave for Government Service

Research Advisory Board

CED Professional and Administrative Staff

Statements on National Policy
Issued by the Research and Policy Committee
(publications in print)

Improving Management of the Public Work Force: The Challenge to State and Local Government *(November 1978)*

Jobs for the Hard-to-Employ: New Directions for a Public-Private Partnership *(January 1978)*

An Approach to Federal Urban Policy *(December 1977)*

Key Elements of a National Energy Strategy *(June 1977)*

The Economy in 1977-78: Strategy for an Enduring Expansion *(December 1976)*

Nuclear Energy and National Security *(September 1976)*

Fighting Inflation and Promoting Growth *(August 1976)*

Improving Productivity in State and Local Government *(March 1976)*

*International Economic Consequences of High-Priced Energy *(September 1975)*

Broadcasting and Cable Television: Policies for Diversity and Change *(April 1975)*

Achieving Energy Independence *(December 1974)*

A New U.S. Farm Policy for Changing World Food Needs *(October 1974)*

Congressional Decision Making for National Security *(September 1974)*

*Toward a New International Economic System:
  A Joint Japanese-American View *(June 1974)*

More Effective Programs for a Cleaner Environment *(April 1974)*

The Management and Financing of Colleges *(October 1973)*

Strengthening the World Monetary System *(July 1973)*

Financing the Nation's Housing Needs *(April 1973)*

Building a National Health-Care System *(April 1973)*

*A New Trade Policy Toward Communist Countries *(September 1972)*

High Employment Without Inflation:
  A Positive Program for Economic Stabilization *(July 1972)*

Reducing Crime and Assuring Justice *(June 1972)*

**Statements issued in association with CED counterpart organizations in
  foreign countries.*

CED Counterpart Organizations
in Foreign Countries

Close relations exist between the Committee for Economic Development and independent, nonpolitical research organizations in other countries. Such counterpart groups are composed of business executives and scholars and have objectives similar to those of CED, which they pursue by similarly objective methods. CED cooperates with these organizations on research and study projects of common interest to the various countries concerned. This program has resulted in a number of joint policy statements involving such international matters as East-West trade, assistance to the developing countries, and the reduction of nontariff barriers to trade.

CEDA Committee for Economic Development of Australia
139 Macquarie Street, Sydney 2001,
New South Wales, Australia

CEPES Europäische Vereinigung für
Wirtschaftliche und Soziale Entwicklung
Reuterweg 14, 6000 Frankfurt/Main, West Germany

IDEP Institut de l'Entreprise
6, rue Clément-Marot, 75008 Paris, France

経済同友会 Keizai Doyukai
(Japan Committee for Economic Development)
Japan Industrial Club Bldg.
1 Marunouchi, Chiyoda-ku, Tokyo, Japan

PSI Policy Studies Institute
12 Upper Belgrave Street, London, SWIX 8BB, England

SNS Studieförbundet Näringsliv och Samhälle
Sköldungagatan, 2, 11427 Stockholm, Sweden